How to
TRAIN YOUR
SKATEBOARD

First published in the United Kingdom in 2023
by Skittledog, an imprint of Thames & Hudson Ltd,
181A High Holborn, London WC1V 7QX

Concept and layout © Thames & Hudson 2023

Text © 2023 Jack Francis
Illustrations © 2023 Ewa Żak

British Library Cataloguing-in-Publication Data
A catalogue record for this book is available
from the British Library

ISBN 978-1-83776-006-0

Printed and bound in China by C&C Printing Offset Co., Ltd

MIX
Paper | Supporting
responsible forestry
FSC® C008047

Be the first to know about our new releases,
exclusive content and author events by visiting
skittledog.com
thamesandhudson.com
thamesandhudsonusa.com
thamesandhudson.com.au

How to TRAIN YOUR SKATEBOARD

JACK FRANCIS

Skittledog

CONTENTS

The Story of
SKATEBOARDING

The exact date of the first skateboard is hard to pin down, but there are reports of people strapping roller-skate wheels to wooden planks as far back as the '40s and '50s. The popularity of skateboarding has been a rollercoaster ride, and it has almost died out on a couple of occasions; however, our favourite recreational activity is still going strong and its inclusion in the Tokyo 2020 and Paris 2024 Olympic Games is a stamp of approval from the mainstream. But how did skateboarding's meteoric rise come about, and what various forms has the board taken on its journey to becoming the one we know and love today?

By the 1960s, skateboarding had been adopted as a hobby by surfers looking to pass the time on quiet days with few waves. The style of skating was heavily influenced by surfing, with barefoot participants mimicking manoeuvres performed on the water, and purpose-built skateboards with wheels made of clay began to be sold. As Californian skaters led the way, dedicated magazines were produced and people exhibited their newfound freestyle skills in competitions, some of which were shown on national television. But then skateboarding saw its first decline: just as it rose, it fell. With metal wheels, fixed trucks and a lack of product development, this iteration of the skateboard provided a frustrating experience. Publications shut down, comps ceased to exist, and the sport was regarded by many as no more than a fad – comparable to the yo-yo.

Fortunately, the '70s saw sidewalk surfing's second wave as a result of major developments in the device's core components. The production of polyurethane, the material that's used to make wheels to this day, led to smoother and quieter rides, and specially designed trucks were fabricated with axles that allowed for steady turns. These advances allowed skaters to acquire their own unique styles which breathed new life into skateboarding. One particular group, the Z-Boys, took the sport by storm as they impressed in both the slalom and freestyle events at the Del Mar contest in 1975. A drought in California in 1976 then led to empty backyard swimming pools being utilised by skaters as they continued to push their abilities to new levels. One notable achievement was that of Z-Boy Tony Alva, who lays claim to the first aerial manoeuvres. This period also saw the first ever skateparks being built, with weird and wonderful designs unlike the parks we've become accustomed to today. But unfortunately the popularity of skating led to an increase in injuries and insurance claims, which eventually led to park closures and, ultimately, a second decline in popularity.

The early 1980s were referred to as the 'dark ages' of skateboarding, but skating wouldn't go down without a fight. The small, thin decks of yesteryear got wider and longer, allowing users to have more control, and a select group of skaters utilised the surviving '70s parks to develop tricks that would become the foundation of modern street skating. Legendary skaters such as Tony Hawk, Mike McGill and Steve Caballero advanced bowl skating to new levels, while freestyle skateboarder Rodney Mullen pushed the boundaries of technical skating by inventing hundreds of tricks – including the flat ground ollie and the kickflip. In 1984 the iconic skate team the Bones Brigade released one of the first widely popular feature-length skate videos, but that film's impact on participation would pale in insignificance to the role of Marty McFly's skateboarding in the 1985 film *Back to the Future*, and many pros would go on to say that the film directly contributed to them picking up a board for the first time.

Vert (short for vertical) skating continued to grow through the '80s, with backyard wooden ramps springing up to make up for the demolition of the old '70s parks, but a large number of people didn't have access to ramps or skateparks and this was the catalyst for the birth of a new form of the sport – street skating. People flocked to urban areas to jump gaps, perform tricks and make the most of street furniture. Mark Gonzales and Natas Kaupas pushed things further by becoming the first skaters to conquer handrails, something that's become a pillar of street skateboarding.

By the '90s skateboards had evolved once again, into the double kick 'popsicle' shape that is predominant today. Being able to skate the board both ways opened up the possibility of doing tricks in the opposite stance, known as skating 'switch'. But despite all this progression, skateboarding experienced its *third* decline as the number of skaters and sales of goods dwindled. However, it would quickly see another revival with the sport appearing in the X Games, an annual extreme sports event which was aired on television globally;

skateboarding had successfully made it back into the mainstream in a big way. This competition series profiled street and vert skating, and would kickstart Tony Hawk's renewed fame which culminated in the release of the *Tony Hawk's Pro Skater* video game - one of the best-selling game series of all time. This brought skating to the masses and made celebrities of the professionals that appeared in it.

Skateboarding's popularity has since been fairly stable, with a huge industry surrounding it. With female participation now up to around 25 per cent and all six women medal winners in the Tokyo Olympics being aged 16 or under, skateboarding has a very bright future too. Now that we all have a camera in our pockets, there's more content out there than ever, and everyone has a chance to shine. Skateboarding may have had its ups and downs over the years, but one thing is for sure - it's here to stay.

Skateboarding has brought so much joy to my life and I'm hoping that by writing this book I can bring some to yours. Whether you intend to skate for fun, to keep fit or to go pro, everything you need to know to get rolling is in these pages. I'll start by taking you through picking your first board, putting it together and choosing where to skate, along with all the other stuff you might need to know to ensure you're as prepared as possible for your first session. Then I'll break down all the basic manoeuvres that form the basis of skateboarding; these are what you'll be doing 90 per cent of the time you're standing on a skateboard. Finally, I'll give you a step-by-step guide to the core tricks that form the foundation for hundreds of other more complex tricks that you may go on to learn.

Getting STARTED

Parts of the
SKATEBOARD

HARDWARE / BOLTS

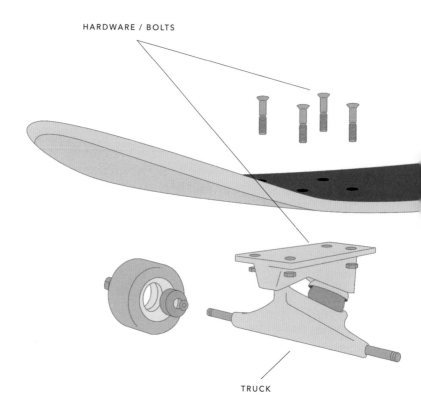

TRUCK

Buying a skateboard can be a daunting prospect, with so many parts made by countless brands in a multitude of shapes, sizes and colours. For beginners it's common to buy it all together, and this is known as a 'complete' or a 'setup'. These can vary drastically in quality and (as with most things) the more you pay, the better the product. Completes at the bottom end of the price range can provide a frustrating experience as they are difficult to turn with; they move slowly and can break easily. When you're starting out, these things can make a big difference to your learning curve.

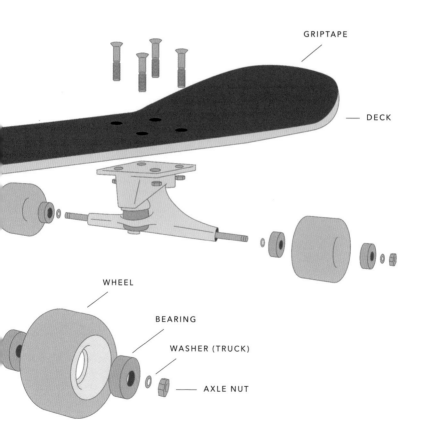

GRIPTAPE

DECK

WHEEL

BEARING

WASHER (TRUCK)

AXLE NUT

As you use your skateboard, things wear down and need to be replaced. This happens to different parts at different rates and buying these bits can be a minefield: the following pages will help you sound like you know what you're talking about when you go into your local skate shop.

Deck

If a skateboard were a band then the deck would be the lead singer, the star of the show. The thing that stands out about this piece of wood is often the graphic printed on the bottom, but this is by no means the most important. These seven pieces of thin maple wood have been squished together and cut with precision.

The deck has a nose and a tail: the nose is at the front and is generally a little longer, while the tail at the back may be closer to the ground. Both of these features make it easier to do tricks.

Size

Decks come in a number of widths ranging from 7 inches to upward of 10. The width you choose is a matter of preference, but generally it's easier for a smaller person to skate a narrower board. If you're very small, or younger than eight or nine, you may want to get a 'mini' deck, which is also shorter in length. If you're small, you could start with a normal-length deck with a width of 7.75 inches and, as you become more comfortable, you can begin experimenting with wider boards.

Shape

Each board has a unique shape and concave. The most common shape is the popsicle, which is used in all styles of skateboarding. There's an array of other deck shapes, generally wider at the tail and near the nose; these tend to have a shorter nose, making tricks more difficult, so it's wise to wait until you've got more experience before giving one a go.

The concave is the curve of the board. Some decks have a mellow concave and are a bit flatter, whereas some have a steep concave. The differences are minute, but some skaters are very particular about which they prefer. The best thing to do when buying a deck is put the board on the ground and stand on it; feeling it under your feet will help you decide what's best for you.

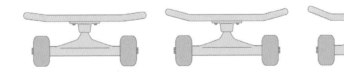

CONCAVES

POPSICLE   SHAPED

Cost

Decks range in price due to a number of factors. At the lower end are 'blank' decks which have no graphic on the underside. Although they are plain, don't turn your nose up at them, especially if you're strapped for cash. They work perfectly well and are often pressed in the same factories and with the same materials as more expensive models. Plus you can cover them in stickers or, if you're feeling particularly creative, come up with your own graphic.

Price also varies depending on the brand. One of the main reasons for this is shipping costs: if you want to save money, buy a deck from a local brand, then you can help support the skateboarding industry in your own country with your purchase.

At the top end of the scale are pro models. When a skateboarder has risen through the ranks and been given a sponsorship by a company, they may gain the honour of going pro and getting their own pro model with their name on. This is a huge achievement for skaters, partly because they receive a percentage of the deck sale. So even though it's a bit pricier, if there's a skater that you really look up to, you can support them by picking up their pro-model deck.

Trucks

These big chunks of metal hold everything together. Generally they last quite a long time, but they are made of a few individual parts that wear down at different rates.

The hanger is the bit that sees most of the action; grind by grind it is slowly scratched away, and this will make grooves in your trucks that will actually help you lock into rails and copings when doing tricks.

Going through the hanger is the axle, to which the wheels are fixed at either end. Sometimes the thread (the spiral groove that allows the nuts to screw on) might be ground off, but your local skate shop will be happy to fix this for you with a tool called a rethreader. At the bottom of the truck is the baseplate, held onto your board by four bolts and extremely sturdy.

Protruding from the baseplate is the kingpin, which holds a number of the essential elements of a truck and has the largest nut of them all on top. Trucks are designed to allow you to turn, and the small rubber bushings found above and below the hanger help this happen. If you find it difficult to turn, then grab a tool and loosen the big nut.

The bushings can come under immense pressure as they take all your weight when you land on your board, so be sure to check they don't split. If something doesn't quite feel right under your feet, then they might be the problem.

The bottom of the hanger sits snugly on the other side of the baseplate and there is another small piece of rubber called a pivot cup that takes a similar amount of pressure as the bushings. Again, this is likely to take some damage, so if your trucks don't turn as they used to then have a look to see if the cups need replacing; they won't cost you much at all.

When buying trucks the main things to consider are the height and the width. How high you want your trucks depends on how big your wheels are. If you buy larger wheels, you'll want to buy higher trucks. The width of your trucks comes down to how wide your deck is – you want them to be fairly similar in width, as this provides the most stability.

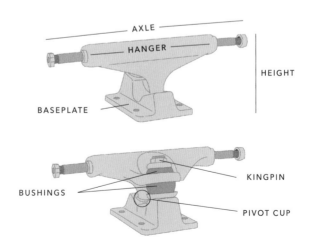

Bearings

Bearings are the unsung hero of the skateboard. Hidden away within the wheel, they are constantly working hard to keep you rolling. The doughnut-shaped casing contains tiny balls made of metal or sometimes ceramic, which reduce friction as the wheels spin.

The quality of the bearing is often measured using the ABEC rating (an industry-standard measure of tolerance), but I wouldn't take much notice of that. Bearings can be found everywhere, and they're essential for making sure some machines don't break down. Those bearings may spin round 30,000 times per minute, so making sure they're made with precision is extremely important. However, unless you intend to ride your skateboard at over 300mph I wouldn't worry about what ABEC your bearings are (the world record speed on a skateboard is currently 91mph).

To keep your board rolling smoothly, buy bearings made by a reputable brand. The worst thing you can do is get your bearings wet as they'll begin to rust, so avoid this at all costs. If they begin to slow, give them a clean and lubricate them, which will get them back to normal.

Bearings are put under significant strain so from time to time one may burst. If this happens you've got two options: either fork out for a whole new set, or you might be lucky enough to find someone with a spare one - either at the skatepark or (if you ask very nicely) at your local skate shop. I always keep a couple spare with me, as there's nothing worse than the session being short.

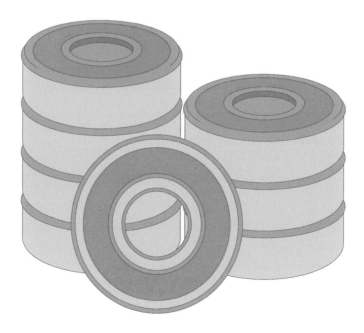

Wheels

This is the one part of a skateboard in constant contact with the ground, working hard to keep you rolling. Wheels come in different shapes, colours and levels of durability, and these variables can impact the speed and manoeuvrability of your board. Your choice will be dictated by what you want to do on your skateboard – whether you prefer skating street or transition, or just want to cruise around.

The first thing to consider is size. The diameter generally starts at around 48mm and can be 60mm or larger at the top end of the scale. The smaller a wheel, the more control you can have over it – they turn more easily and are lighter, making flip tricks less strenuous. It's also a little easier to balance on them, particularly for smaller people. However, this does come at the cost of being slower than their larger counterparts.

Diameter

Larger wheels are the go-to for vert and bowl skaters as their ability to maintain speed is perfect for this style of skating. Note that the larger the wheel the higher the risk of wheel bite, which is when the wheel comes into contact with the board, causing it to stop moving. To prevent this you can put risers on your board; a thin piece of plastic that goes in between the trucks and the deck, increasing the height of the truck and the clearance between the wheels and the board. If you're not sure what size to go for, then 54mm is a good all-rounder.

For longboards and cruisers, wheels get even bigger. This helps you travel smoothly over rough terrain. The chances of hitting a small stone and flying through the air drop significantly when you've got wheels that can roll straight over it.

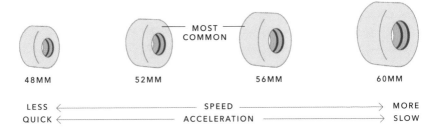

| 48MM | 52MM | 56MM | 60MM |

LESS ← SPEED → MORE
QUICK ← ACCELERATION → SLOW

SOFT ⟵———————————————⟶ HARD

73A   80A   85A   101A

MORE ⟵————————— GRIP —————————⟶ LESS

Durability

The next thing to consider is the durability of your wheels. The softer the wheel, the more easily it travels over the ground and the smoother the ride you'll have. The harder the wheel, the faster it will go. Harder wheels may have less grip, but they enable you to powerslide and allow for more precise control. If a wheel is too soft it may make it more difficult to pop certain tricks, but they are perfect for cruising on. A durometer is used to measure the durability of wheels; the softest wheels start at 73a, and the scale goes up to 101a. If you're unsure what to get, then a wheel that's 96a-99a is a good place to start, as it gives you the best of both worlds.

Contact

The final thing to consider is the wheel shape and the resulting size of the contact patch (this is the part of the wheel that is in contact with the ground). The larger the contact patch, the more grip you have - even when going at high speeds, If you're looking to go fast and maintain control, then a wider wheel is best for you. If you favour manoeuvrability and keeping your deck light, then go for the more classic wheel shape with a narrower contact.

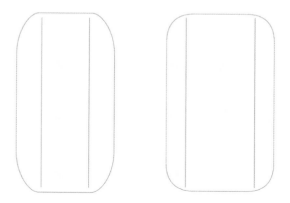

Putting your
BOARD TOGETHER

Even if you buy a complete, at some point you're going to want to replace parts of your setup. Therefore, it's essential you know how to take apart and put together the different components of your skateboard.

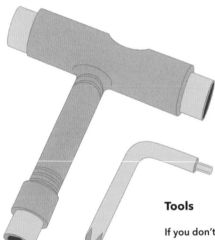

Tools

If you don't already have lots of tools then I recommend getting a T tool. This handy bit of kit comes with exactly what you need to tighten and loosen the three nut sizes found on a standard skateboard. It may also come with an Allen key to hold the bolts in place as you unscrew them. Some bolts need a screwdriver instead of an Allen key, so check to see whether your tool also has a Phillips head on the Allen key. It may even come with a part for rethreading worn-down trucks and another part for putting bearings in wheels, but you have to splash out for that.

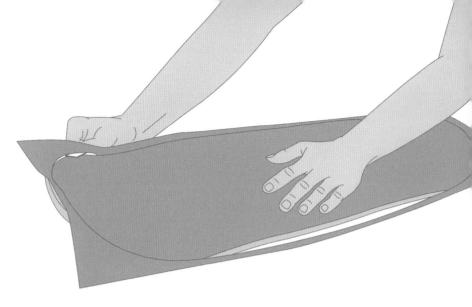

Gripping your board

The part of a skateboard that's most commonly replaced tends to be the deck. When you buy a new deck, the skate shop worker may put the grip on for you, but if they don't, or if you buy online, then you'll need to grip it yourself.

First off you need to peel off the paper from the back of the grip. Put it aside as you'll need it in a moment. Place the grip over the deck gently, being careful to make sure it's straight over the board and covering it entirely, but don't stick it down fully yet. Grab the paper from before, and place it on top of the grip, then rub your hands across it, pressing down while pushing out any air bubbles. Start in the centre of the board and push outwards.

Now you need to trim the edges and get rid of the excess grip. To make it easier to cut and get a clean finish, use a long, hard metal object (a file or a spanner works well) and scrape it round the edges of the board.

Once you've got a clear line going round the edge of your board, cut the excess off. This involves using a sharp

object, so if you're young or a bit clumsy ask someone to help you out. You're going to need a sharp blade like a Stanley knife or razor blade. Run the blade along the edge of the board, slicing off the grip. Be careful not to pull the blade in case it slips.

Once it's all been chopped off, you can use a bit of the excess grip to smooth off the edges. Fold it in half so it doesn't get stuck to your fingers, and rub it around the side of the grip/deck. This should stop it from peeling off. All that's left to do is poke through the holes; use a screwdriver or one of your bolts to press through the grip from the underside of the deck and repeat.

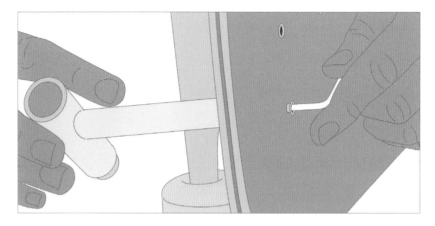

Changing trucks

Trucks are fixed to the deck with eight bolts, so you first need to take them off. Lay your skateboard on its side, place the smallest socket of your tool over one of the nuts and put the Allen key or screwdriver into the top of the bolt. Twist the tool anti-clockwise (righty tighty, lefty loosey) while holding the bolt in place until the bolt comes off. Get the bolt out and repeat this until both trucks are off.

When putting the trucks on a deck you might find it useful to push all the bolts through the holes, place the truck on and screw the bolts on a little by hand, then tighten them all up with the tool. Double-check that you've got your trucks on the right way, with the kingpins toward the centre of the board, before you tighten them. Make sure you don't screw them on too tightly or you'll damage the wood and increase the likelihood of snapping your deck. The head of the bolt should be even with the griptape.

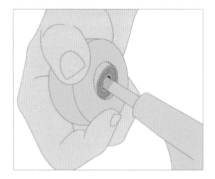

Changing wheels

To remove the wheel you need to take off the axle nut. Place the medium-sized socket on your tool over the nut and twist it anti-clockwise. If you need to remove the bearings, hold the wheel and put about a centimetre of the axle of your truck through the bearing, then twist the wheel so the axle catches on the bearing. You should be able to get enough purchase to pull the bearing off. Repeat this with the bearing on the other side of the wheel.

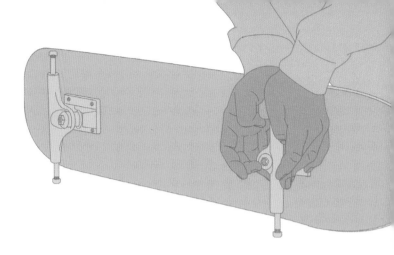

Changing bearings

You're also going to use your trucks as a tool to get the bearings into your wheels. Put one bearing onto the truck axle, ensuring that the part that goes on the outside of the wheel is facing down. Put the wheel onto the axle and push down so that the truck forces the bearing into the wheel. Now repeat with the second bearing, making sure you turn the wheel so the bearing can go into the empty part of the wheel. Once you've replaced all the bearings in your wheels you can put them back on. If you've got washers (small metal rings that help the wheel spin), make sure you put one on before each wheel and one on after. Screw the nut onto the wheel a little by hand and then use your tool to tighten it. Make sure you tighten to the point that the wheel wiggles about, but not so much that it doesn't spin round.

Adjusting trucks

Before you set off for a skate you may want to adjust how tight your trucks are. Place the largest socket of your tool over the kingpin nut in the centre of your truck and twist it clockwise to tighten it, or anti-clockwise to loosen it. This will affect your board's ability to turn and the level of stability you have. If you completely remove the kingpin nut, then you can pull the truck apart. This will allow you to replace your bushings and pivot cup.

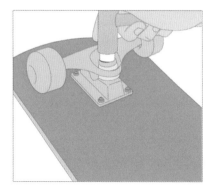

What to
WEAR

Once your board is good to go you're almost ready to head out for a skate, but before you do, you'll need to decide what to wear. Skate culture has been trendsetting for years, and skateparks can often feel like a fashion parade. Despite this, think twice about wearing your freshest threads because they'll be up against it when you're sliding along concrete. Whatever you wear, make sure it's something you won't mind putting a hole in or getting covered in dirt.

Pads

If you're learning how to skate then you need to become familiar with falling on the ground. Knee pads, elbow pads, wrist guards and a helmet are crucial for ensuring you skate safely while finding your feet. Over 30 per cent of injuries occur in the first four weeks of skateboarding, so don't feel embarrassed about wearing protective equipment because this is the most vulnerable point in your skateboarding journey.

Footwear

Choosing footwear can be tough with such a broad selection out there, but whatever you pick, don't get too attached to them because they will inevitably get ruined. The constant scraping of your shoes against your board's griptape will grind them down until your toes poke out, but there are things that will make your shoes last longer. Skate-specific shoes are designed to be able to withstand the trials of skateboarding and will provide you with the comfort, grip and board-feel required to skate well while taking big impacts.

That's not to say that every skate shoe will be well designed, but it's a good place to start. Certain materials will last longer than others – canvas and soft leather will be torn to shreds relatively easily, so watch out. Suede, toughened leather and some synthetic materials are much more durable and will save you money in the long run.

Helmet

If there's one part of your body you'll want to protect most, it's your head. You'll notice that almost all skaters wear helmets when skating vert, as the risk level increases when hitting bigger ramps. If you're skating something bigger than you're used to, consider putting a lid on, for protection or to get the confidence to do something that pushes your limits.

Make sure you get a helmet that's designed specifically for skateboarding. A bicycle helmet, for example, is designed to take impacts from the front, whereas a skateboard helmet is constructed to take impacts from all directions
.

Trousers/shorts

What you should wear on the bottom half of your body is another contested topic in the world of skateboarding. The legwear of choice for most skateboarders is jeans. Loose-fitting trousers provide both comfort and protection from scrapes and bruises. It's undeniable that a thin layer of cotton can be the difference between keeping the skin on your shins or losing it to some concrete. A long pair of thick socks may also help reduce the damage inflicted on your legs, especially by your board when doing flip tricks or when skating street. If you're going to go bare legged then a pair of thick socks is advisable, and if you're not already wearing knee pads then you may want to reconsider.

HELMET

ELBOW PADS

WRIST GUARDS

KNEE PADS

Where to SKATE

The beauty of skateboarding is that all you need is your board and some flat ground and you're good to go. When I learned to skate, my friends and I spent hours on a quiet street round the corner from my house. All we had was a smooth bit of road and a couple of curbs, and it was enough to keep us entertained for hours on end. But at some point you might want to venture beyond your local area to places that will push your ability.

Public skateparks

Skateparks are a great place to get started. All the obstacles are designed to simulate things that can be found in urban areas but will be smoother and sturdier than those found in the wild. They're clear of traffic and are usually well maintained so they're relatively safe to skate in comparison to a crusty ledge next to a main road in the city centre. Parks and the ramps within them tend to be made of concrete, wood or occasionally metal. Each material is good for skating, but there are some things to be aware of. Unsurprisingly, concrete is hard and a heavy slam on it can shake you up. Wooden ramps are a bit more forgiving when you fall, but they may be more slippery than other materials.

Private skateparks

While the majority of outdoor skateparks are built and owned publicly, some outdoor parks and most indoor ones are privately owned, and you may have to pay for entry. This might include having to register and pre-book a specific time slot. Despite the fact that skating at most indoor skateparks will cost you, they come with the huge benefit of being protected from the elements.

Indoor alternatives

If you're short on cash or the indoor park is packed then you'll need to find an alternative place to skate. Anywhere with a roof will do, but unfortunately, covered areas where you can skate aren't easy to come by and have their downsides. Car parks are an option – they have flat ground, curbs, manual pads and sometimes even stairs and rails – but they come with two main disadvantages: firstly, they're full of cars, which can obviously be a real hazard if you're not careful; secondly, they are often attended by security who may kick you out within minutes of your arrival. It's not ideal.

Street skating

Another option is to skate street, and some argue that this is skateboarding in its purest form. The built environment is full of skateable objects: you can find banks, rails, stairs, ledges and all manner of other concrete blocks that can be repurposed as skateboarding obstacles. Some of the most famous skateboarding spots in the world aren't skateparks at all, but something that was built for a completely different purpose and has become part of skateboarding heritage due to the opportunism of skateboarders who see urban areas in a different way from the rest of the population. If you want to skate street but don't know where to start, try asking people at your local skatepark or search onlne for cities' hidden spots.

Types of OBSTACLES

Skateparks are packed full of differently shaped bits of wood, metal and concrete for you to skate on. These objects can be skated in different ways and have various names - sometimes it can feel like a whole new language in itself. So, here's a brief guide to what you can expect to encounter at a skatepark and on the streets.

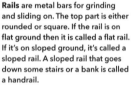

Rails are metal bars for grinding and sliding on. The top part is either rounded or square. If the rail is on flat ground then it is called a flat rail. If it's on sloped ground, it's called a sloped rail. A sloped rail that goes down some stairs or a bank is called a handrail.

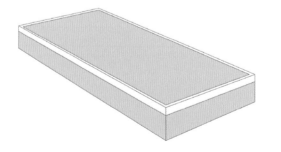

Grind boxes are boxes with edges that you can grind on; they may be concrete or wooden with metal edges but are sometimes marble, which is a particularly nice material for grinding. A very low grind box is called a manual (manny) pad, as it's a good height for doing manuals on. If a grind box is particularly narrow or connected to the side of another ramp it may be called a ledge. When a ledge is sloped it's called a hubba; these normally go alongside stairs or a bank.

Kicker/launch ramps can be either angled or curved and are used for getting air off. They tend to be smaller than most ramps and can be portable.

Flatbanks, or banks as they're commonly called, are angled ramps that you can roll in from the top of or go up and do tricks on.

Quarter pipes are ramps with a curved transition from the flat ground. They usually have a metal bar called coping at the top. When two quarter pipes are connected and facing opposite each other this is called a halfpipe, but if it's not very tall and not vertical at the top then it's called a mini ramp. Two back-to-back quarter pipes are called a spine.

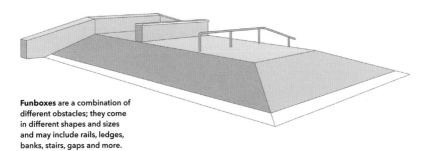

Funboxes are a combination of different obstacles; they come in different shapes and sizes and may include rails, ledges, banks, stairs, gaps and more.

Hips are where two ramps meet so that the adjoining part is protruding outwards. These could be two flatbanks, two quarter pipes or even part of a bowl. The two ramps may meet to form a clear edge, or they may blend into each other seamlessly.

Bowls/pools can either be purpose built for skateboarding, or just an emptied swimming pool. Park skateboarding competitions take place in bowls, and they vary in size and shape. Even purpose-built bowls may include features of swimming pools, such as concrete pool coping, a strip of mosaic tiling near the coping or 'deathboxes' – the rectangular gap near the coping that would contain the pool drain.

Skatepark ETIQUETTE

DON'T OVER-WAX

SNAKING

BEING AWARE
OF THE LINE

DON'T BE
ANNOYING

Skateparks can be daunting places, especially when you're starting out. You might worry that you'll get in someone's way or do something wrong, but you needn't worry. It doesn't matter how good you are at skating; once you know the unwritten rules of how to use a skatepark you can roll around carefree, confident that you're not going to upset anyone. After all, you're just as entitled to skate there as anyone else is, especially if you maintain perfect skatepark etiquette.

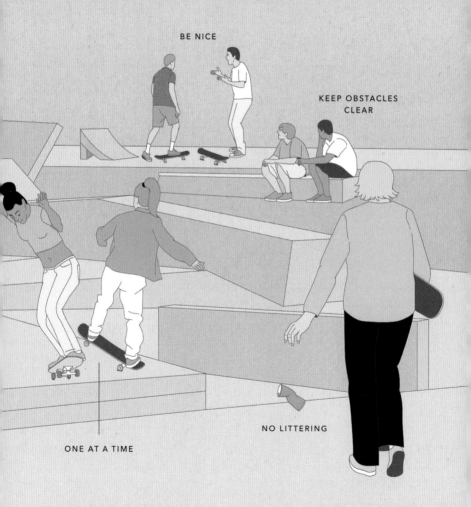

BE NICE

KEEP OBSTACLES CLEAR

ONE AT A TIME

NO LITTERING

Skatepark
ETIQUETTE

No snaking When you get to the top of a ramp you're at the back of the queue and must wait for the others to go before it's your turn. You're not just in a queue with the people on that ramp but also other ramps in that line, so make sure there's no one waiting to come from the other direction. Even if you're the best skater in the park, you still have to wait your turn. Don't jump the queue, snaking won't make you any friends.

Be aware of the lines You need to be very aware of what's going on around you, so you don't crash into anyone. Generally, people will go to and from specific points in the park, especially in parks with more of a street layout; these paths are called lines. This means that skateboarding traffic will be flowing steadily along certain routes, so if you're going to cross a line then make sure no one is coming, and if you want to skate then be sure to follow the lines or be extra careful.

Keep obstacles clear Almost everything in a park is built to be skated, so try to keep it clear. Put your belongings out of the way, but keep an eye on them. There's nothing more annoying than people sitting on an obstacle you're trying to skate; if you do this then prepare to be shouted at or crashed into. Even if you're about to go down a ramp, make sure you stay well clear of the edge until it's your turn, so as not to obstruct anyone.

One at a time If a skatepark is empty and it's just you and your crew, then feel free to all hit the lines together, it's good fun. But if the park is busy, only go one at a time. If someone has just gone down a ramp then wait until they're done before you take your turn. Keep the risk of collisions to a minimum and let everyone have their fair share of the park.

Don't over-wax Wax is perfect for making sticky surfaces grindable, but don't go overboard. Too much wax can turn metal into black ice and make an obstacle unskateable, or even get someone hurt. The easy way around this is to wax your trucks and board. If you really feel that something needs waxing then ask other skaters if they mind you waxing it; it's common courtesy and more often than not, they will oblige.

No littering When doing a sport in which a tiny stone can send you flying off your board, it's super important to keep the place clear of rubbish. So don't throw litter on the ground, whether you're at a skatepark, a local spot, in the street, or anywhere: just don't do it!

Be nice Skateparks are places where people with a mutual love for skateboarding (and BMXing and roller-skating) can come together. It's a place for people to learn, chat, express themselves and have a good time. So try to be a part of making it a place where others can enjoy themselves. If someone is struggling then offer them help.

Don't be annoying If someone is trying a trick, or has just landed a trick that they had been trying for a long time, don't do that trick straight away as you may come across as a show-off. Also, don't give people unsolicited advice, it can come across as condescending. Instead, ask if they would like a tip and give them the opportunity to accept or turn down your offer.

Basic SKILLS

Standing on
YOUR BOARD

To maximise your chances of staying on your board, it's important that you have the right foot position. In fact, foot position is something you need to consider a lot when skating, as you'll need to set up differently in order to do certain tricks. But for now, let's focus on where to have your feet when simply rolling around.

Regular or goofy

First you need to decide which foot goes forward. Skateboarders are either regular, meaning their left foot is at the front, or goofy, with their right foot at the front. This doesn't seem to be connected to being left- or right-handed, or left- or right-footed in other sports, it's just what you find most comfortable. If you're not sure, then try both stances and one will feel a little more natural than the other.

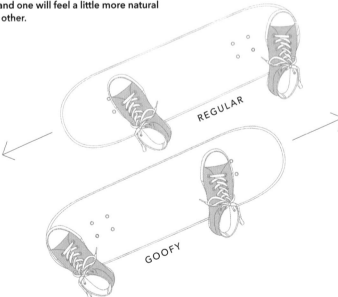

REGULAR

GOOFY

Stance

When stepping onto your board, place your front foot over the bolts and your back foot on the tail. It's good to keep your feet as wide apart as possible, as a wide base helps you to balance and will reduce the chances of you falling off. Make sure your feet are sideways on the board and your knees are slightly bent, giving you a lower centre of gravity which will allow you to readjust your balance more easily.

There are some other important terms that refer to how you stand on your skateboard. If you skate the opposite way to the one natural to you (e.g. you're regular but skate goofy), this is known as switch. If you move from your natural foot position up onto the nose of the board, this is known as nollie. If you stand in your natural position, but go backwards, this is known as fakie.

FALLING

If you want to get into skateboarding, then you have to accept the inevitability that you are going to fall over. Even professionals, who spend almost every waking hour of the day skateboarding, have to pick themselves up off the ground.

But don't let the idea of bailing cloud your mind with worry: being too preoccupied by the fact that you might fall over is only going to hold you back. Fortunately, there are ways of falling onto the ground that lead to no physical harm whatsoever, and learning them sooner rather than later is advisable.

Falling onto your knees

It's definitely recommended to pad up when learning to skate, but knee pads in particular can be your saving grace when it comes to falling over. They can give you the perfect escape route if you ever feel like you're losing balance, or aren't going to land back on your board.

To start off with, once you've got your knee pads on, practise dropping onto your knees. If it hurts at all then you might want to check you've got your pads on correctly and that they are the right size. If it doesn't hurt then have a go at a knee slide. If you're at a skatepark, you can practise falling onto your knees on an uneven surface. If you've got knee, elbow and wrist protection on, then you can practise falling off your board onto all fours.

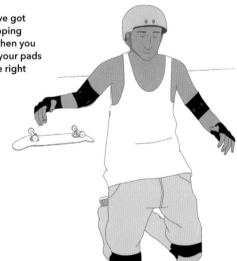

Falling without landing on your hands

In an ideal world you'd always be able to fall painlessly onto your knees, but unfortunately, sometimes things don't pan out that way. And for those of you that prefer not to wear pads, an impact to the knees wouldn't be ideal. So what are the other options? One of the main issues when coming off your board is that most people's initial reaction is to put their hands out to break their fall; however, hands and wrists aren't very robust, so you won't be surprised to hear that wrists, along with ankles, are the most commonly injured part of the body when skating. In light of this, it's important to find a way of falling without sacrificing the many bones joining your hands to your arms.

Fortunately, your shoulders and the side of your upper body can provide the cushioning necessary to break your fall. As you come off your board, try to point your hands away from the ground, and pull them into your body, this will help you take the impact on the side of your body. The faster you're moving, the easier this becomes, as you can slide along the ground. Obviously this method of falling comes at the cost of your clothing, especially your T-shirts, but it's a small price to pay.

PUSHING

Now that you can stand on your board and know how to fall off it, you'll want to start moving about. Unless you're on a hill, this will require pushing, which involves keeping one foot on your deck, while applying pressure with your other foot against the ground before hoisting it onto your board.

Starting position

To begin with, you need to place your front foot on the skateboard pointing forward, over the bolts of the front truck. It shouldn't be so far forward that putting pressure on your toes causes the back wheels to come off the ground - this would make things very awkward. Your back foot should be on the ground next to it, also facing forward. Make sure your foot is quite close to the skateboard but not so close it will clip the wheels.

Movement

Use your foot on the ground to push your skateboard and front foot forward. As your back foot nears the tail of your board, lift it up and place it on the tail, sideways onto the board. As you put your back foot on, rotate your shoulders so that instead of facing forward, your body is now side-on. When you're doing the pushing motion, make sure that your back foot starts alongside your front foot and not too far back. If you want to do more than one push before putting your foot back on the board, make sure you get your foot back alongside your front foot before repeating the pushing motion.

Final foot placement/movement

Now that both feet are on the board you need to get back into the standard, stable foot position. Twist your front foot so that, along with your back foot, it's sideways on the board. Your griptape might make changing your foot position tricky, but if you lift your heel up, so only your toes are in contact with your board, it should make it a little easier. Each time you want to push you will have to twist your front foot so it faces forward again. If you prefer, you can keep your front foot in a diagonal position that allows you to twist from pushing to standing without moving your front foot too much.

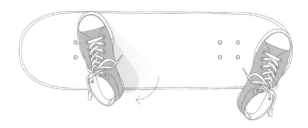

Pushing while moving/ pushing faster

To really maximise the power of each push you can bend your legs and extend them with each push. To go even faster, start each pushing movement with your leg extended forwards, allowing you to do longer, harder pushes. One way to improve your pushes is to practise balancing on your front leg, with your foot on the bolts, pointing forward, and mimic the motion of doing big pushes with your back leg, but without putting your foot on the ground. This will help build up your strength and balance.

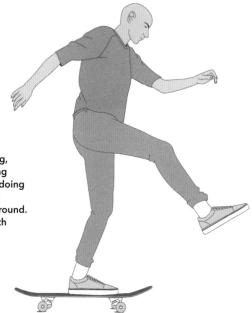

Mongo

Some people find it easier to push with their front foot while having their back foot pointing forward on the back truck bolts; this is referred to as pushing mongo. While this is acceptable, there are a few things to consider. Firstly, this requires more repositioning of the feet as you have to twist your back foot and get it back on the tail before being able to ollie or do most tricks. Secondly, your skateboard will be a little more unstable, especially if you're going quite fast.

Without any of your weight on the front truck it's much easier to slip out or lose control of the front of the board. Finally, and rather unfortunately, pushing mongo has become a bit of a skateboarding faux pas, mainly because it's hard to push this way without it appearing a bit uncomfortable. Even though skateboarding claims to

celebrate individuality and embrace quirks, unfortunately pushing mongo is somewhat frowned upon and you might get some funny looks if you do it.

If you're reading this as someone who's just starting out or hasn't been skating for long, my advice would be to learn to push with your back foot. However, if you're reading this as a person who has pushed this way for a while then I wouldn't worry about it; there's no wrong way to skate, and as long as you're enjoying yourself and it's not holding you back then there's no need to change.

1

2

STOPPING

Once you're moving you're eventually going to want to come to a stop. There are a few different ways to do this that vary in terms of ease, practicality and style.

Place foot on ground (1)

The simplest way to stop is essentially the same method used to push, but in reverse. Twist your front foot so it's facing forward, take your back foot off the board and place it flat on the ground. You'll need to place it slightly behind your front foot and stiffen your leg, as you'll meet some resistance. How much resistance depends on how fast you're going and how smooth the ground is.

If you're finding this tricky then there's always the option of jumping straight off your board and landing on the ground with both feet. You will want to learn to stop with your foot on the ground at some point though.

Tail scrape (2)

This brings you to a halt by dragging the end of the board on the ground. As you're moving along with your feet in the standard foot position, lift up your front foot by bending your front leg, and lower your back foot by straightening your back leg. This position is like standing on one leg while on your skateboard. This will push the tail down to the ground, creating enough friction to slow you down. Try to keep your shoulders over the board; if you lean too far back, you'll fall off.

Powerslide

Powersliding involves turning your body and skateboard 90 degrees and moving while your wheels scrape against the ground. It's definitely the most graceful and efficient way to stop or slow down. Whether you're trying to keep your speed in check as you're bombing it down a hill, or need to make an emergency stop to avoid crashing into something, powersliding is your best bet, although it's worth noting that this skill takes some perfecting. You may find it easier to learn on a smooth, flat surface – you need considerably more speed when doing it on rough ground, and if you don't get it quite right you'll end up either sliding on your bum or being ejected forward, neither of which are ideal when hurtling down a steep, gravelly road.

Start off by getting a good amount of speed, getting your feet into the standard position and bending your knees. Then rotate your shoulders, lean back and extend your back leg as you rotate your hips, so that the back truck moves alongside the front truck – you should now be facing forward.

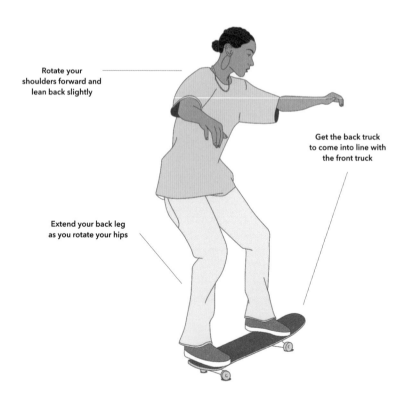

Rotate your shoulders forward and lean back slightly

Get the back truck to come into line with the front truck

Extend your back leg as you rotate your hips

Once you're in the powersliding position, it's really important that you lean back enough to match the resistance from the ground against your wheels. You can even dig your heels in and raise your toes slightly to help push the board along. Lean back too little and the board will grind to a halt, too much and you'll fall on your bum. As you begin to slow down you've got two options: either bend your back knee, rotate shoulders and hips, and lean forward a little to return to your normal stance, or let the skateboard come to a complete stop, making sure to lean a little forward just before you're stationary so you don't fall back.

Working this manoeuvre out will take some trial and error with the speed you need to be at and how much to lean back, but once you've got the hang of it you'll be doing it non-stop – it's good fun. Try going really fast and see how long you can do one. Be careful, though: you run the risk of flat-spotting your wheels, especially if they're brand new. This is when you wear down a bit of your wheel, making it flat compared to the rest; if it's particularly bad then it will make an awful noise when you're rolling and slow you down. You've been warned!

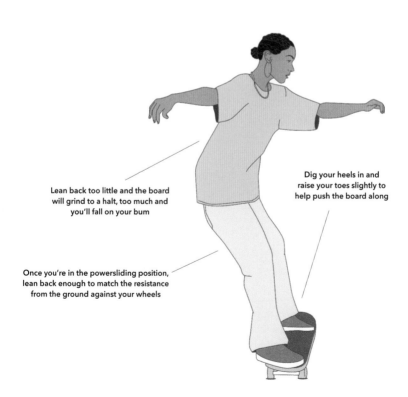

Lean back too little and the board will grind to a halt, too much and you'll fall on your bum

Dig your heels in and raise your toes slightly to help push the board along

Once you're in the powersliding position, lean back enough to match the resistance from the ground against your wheels

TURNING

There are two ways to turn on a skateboard, and each method is appropriate for different situations. The most basic way requires far less effort and is better when going at speed, as you have more control over the board because all four wheels stay on the ground. Turning this way is possible due to the way that trucks are made: the bushings allow the axle to move, and you can see this in action if you turn your board over and push down on one of the wheels. Putting pressure on either side of the deck allows you to move in that direction.

To do this type of turn well, it is important to have your feet in the standard foot position. This is so that you can use your heels and toes to apply pressure to the left and right sides of your board. Whether this makes you go left or right depends on whether you're regular or goofy.

When moving, to turn in one direction, lean forward over the edge of your board, and push down on your toes

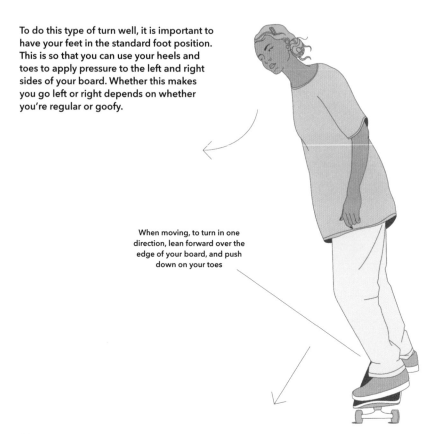

REMEMBER

If your board doesn't seem to turn very well, there are a couple of things you can do. First, double-check your foot position; if your front foot is pointing forward then you'll find this particularly difficult. The second thing you can do is loosen your trucks. Grab your tool and loosen the kingpin bolt, which should allow your trucks to move a little more freely. It's also worth noting that this will be a lot easier if you are heavier, as you can exert more pressure on the board and get the trucks to respond more easily. If you're small, don't worry, there's another way to turn (see over the page).

You can raise your arms and use them to help you balance

To turn the other way, lean back and apply pressure to the edge of the board using your heels

Kick
TURNS

This method of turning allows you to change direction much more quickly and is the turn of preference when going up and down ramps. It's done by lifting up the front of the board and pivoting on the back truck. It requires a little more balance than the simple turn but it's extremely useful. We'll begin by learning to do it stationary and then progress to doing it while moving.

The foot position is the same as usual but pay extra attention to where your back foot is - the further down the tail it is, the more control you'll have over raising and lowering the front truck. Keep your legs bent, as this will aid your balance and allow you to lift up/push down the board with your feet. This manoeuvre, along with others in which you and your board spin together, starts with your upper body.

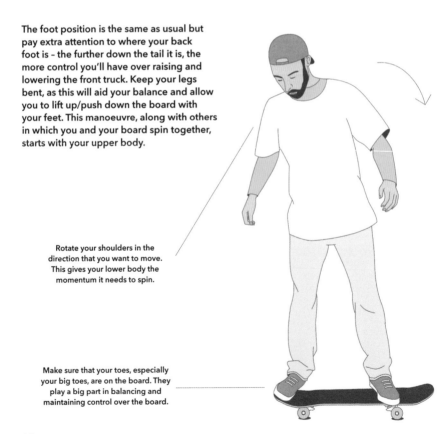

Rotate your shoulders in the direction that you want to move. This gives your lower body the momentum it needs to spin.

Make sure that your toes, especially your big toes, are on the board. They play a big part in balancing and maintaining control over the board.

Don't lean back when you pivot on your back foot. Keep your back shoulder over your back truck or you might fall off your board.

As the top half of your body starts to move, the bottom half needs to kick into action. At this point you need to lift up your front truck. Sometimes people struggle to get the front truck up, especially if they're smaller. If that's the case, you may want to bring your front foot slightly further down the board, towards the centre.

Once you've pivoted and your front foot has caught up with your shoulders, put your front truck back down on the ground. Keep practising this until you feel confident enough to do it moving. Remember that you need to practise this in both directions, even if doing it frontside is a little more difficult than backside.

Lift your front truck by straightening your back leg as you bend your front leg

Twist your shoulders and raise your front foot

To do a kick turn while moving it's necessary to do a combination of the two turns together – doing *only* a kick turn will lead to you falling off your skateboard. You might need to do lots of little kick turns if you wish to perform a large change of direction. The faster you're going, the smaller each movement will need to be.

Lean in the direction you wish to turn

Get your feet in position

Push to get some speed

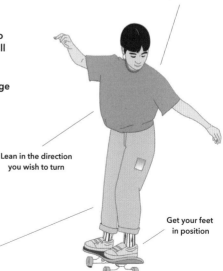

ROLLING IN

Rolling in is when you go down a ramp from the top by rolling into it. The first ramp you will want to try this on is a bank. The difficulty will depend entirely on how big and steep the bank is, but the overall technique is the same no matter the size. When standing on your skateboard on flat ground you can stand straight up and maintain balance with relative ease; when you're standing on your skateboard on a sloped surface this isn't the case, and you have to redistribute your weight in order to remain standing on your board.

How you get enough speed to roll into the ramp will depend on how much space you have at the top. If you have a large amount of space then make the most of it. Push off from a distance so you have time to get your feet in the standard foot position before going over the top. You may have very little space at the top of the ramp but may be able to get your feet in position and then jiggle them a little, so your front wheels go over the edge. You may even have a wall or barrier that you can push off in order to get down the ramp.

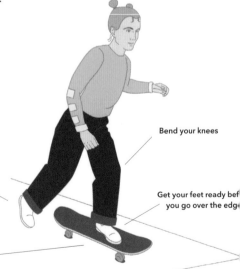

Place your back foot on the tail and your front foot over the bolts for optimal balance

Redistribute your weight to stay balanced on an uneven surface. As your front wheels go over the edge of the top of the bank you'll begin to roll down, so if you stay standing upright your board will shoot forward without you. To prevent this, you need to lean forward.

Bend your knees

Get your feet ready bef
you go over the edg

Once you get to the transition from sloped to flat you need to redistribute your weight again. As you reach the flat, bend your back leg so that you're standing upright again. If you're going down a big, steep ramp then you'll need to bend both legs to absorb the shock of the transition and ensure you stay balanced.

REMEMBER

Sometimes when the back truck goes over the top of the ramp it makes people bend their back leg. It's really important you don't let this happen or you'll fall backwards.

Keep your back leg more extended than your front leg so that you stay leaning forward

Straighten your back leg slightly and bend your front leg - this will cause the top half of your body to move over the front of the skateboard, keeping it firmly under your feet

On a steeper ramp you'll need to lean further forward to stay on your board

Going up
A RAMP

Going up a ramp is just like going down one but in reverse; however, the technique differs depending on the ramp that you're going up. We'll begin by looking at going up a bank, which is a bit simpler.

Going up a bank

Just as when you go down a bank, in order to maintain balance and stay standing on your board you need to shift your weight by moving the top half of your body. As you approach the ramp make sure your knees are bent and your feet are on the tail and the front bolts. As your front wheels reach the bottom of the ramp you need to lean back by bending your back leg a little and extending your front leg. If it's a particularly steep ramp then you'll need to lean further back. Make sure your body is sideways on the board, along with your feet; if your body is facing forwards, it will be quite difficult to balance once you start coming down the ramp backwards.

Once you're up the ramp you'll come to a stop - at this point turn your head and look down the ramp in the direction you're heading, which will help with balance

You'll now roll down the ramp backwards. When you get to the transition from slope to flat, readjust your legs and the way you're leaning so you're standing upright, bending your knees to absorb any shock.

Banks and quarter pipes

These require a different approach. On a bank you adjust your body position once to go from flat to sloped; however, quarter pipes become steeper the higher up you go. When going up a quarter pipe you need to continue to lean further back the higher up you go. If the quarter pipe is vertical at the top, you'll need to lean back 90 degrees to stay on your board.

Bend your knees as you get higher up the ramp to help you maintain balance

DROPPING IN

When you go down a bank you can just roll straight in, but as a quarter pipe has coping, rolling in becomes more difficult because your trucks can get caught. Dropping in is the manoeuvre that's best for getting down a quarter pipe. Instead of rolling, you rest your board on the edge of the ramp before leaning forward and rolling down. Learning this is always a big moment in your skateboarding journey, and as you gain confidence you can take it onto bigger ramps. Quarter pipes can be different heights and gradients, and can have differently shaped transitions, so learning to drop in on different ones can sometimes feel like learning to do it all over again.

This is likely to be one of the scariest things you've done on a skateboard so far, so it might be useful to have a friend to help you. They can support you by putting their hands under your elbows while you hold on to their arms. Try not to just hold on to their hands as they won't be able to support you that much and you might end up hurting each other.

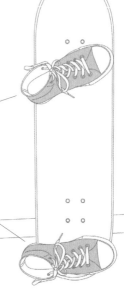

Your front foot should be over the bolts, and both should be in a sideways position. When resting in this position, you should have almost all your weight on your back leg.

Place your board over the coping so the back truck is over the edge of the ramp with the wheels resting against the coping - your back foot will keep the board in place.

As you know from going up a quarter pipe, when you're rolling into the ramp, you need to redistribute your weight in order to stay on your board. When you're on the steepest part of the ramp you need to lean quite a lot to do this. This means that when you drop in you're presented with the challenge of shifting your weight from an upright position to leaning quite far forward. The other difficulty to overcome is that as soon as you put pressure on your front foot, you and your board will start to go down the ramp.

The top half of your body should be facing slightly forwards and your knees bent

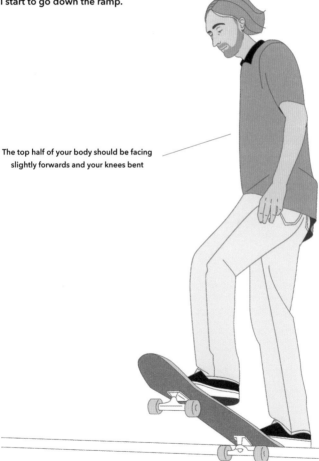

Move your shoulders forward and
downward while keeping your feet
and board in the same position

Bend your knees a little when
getting in position at the top
of the ramp

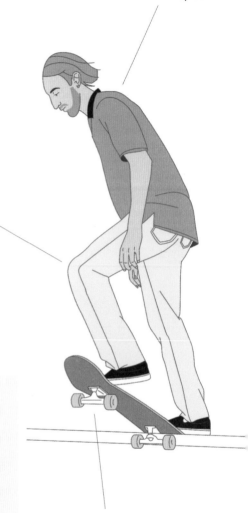

REMEMBER

Make sure that you're looking down
at the ground beyond the nose of your
skateboard as this is where the top half
of your body needs to go. Then, with
your hand which is closer to the nose
of your board, try to reach past your
nose before slamming your front truck
down. If you can put your hand beyond
your board's nose, you'll be able to get
your shoulders where they need to be.

Once the top half of your body is far
enough in the ramp, slam down your
front foot so your board starts moving
down the ramp

You now need to focus on landing on your board and getting down the ramp. Extend your front leg so you slam the front truck onto the ramp and bend your legs to take the impact. If you've leaned forward enough you should roll down the ramp. If you slip back then you've not got your body far enough into the ramp, so dust yourself off and give it another go.

Kick Turns
ON RAMPS

Once you've gained some confidence going up and down ramps, you'll be ready to start challenging yourself on them. A really useful thing to be able to do is turn around while on a ramp instead of just coming back down fakie. This means combining three movements: twisting your shoulders, raising your front truck and redistributing your weight so you stay on your board.

To make this move a little easier to begin with, I recommend approaching the ramp at an angle, making sure your body is facing away from the ramp when you approach it, as backside kick turns are much easier than frontside ones. You can also try this quite low down on the ramp to gain some confidence, then get a bit more speed to go higher up it.

If you're starting from the flat then do a couple of pushes and get your feet on the board, giving yourself enough time to get them in position before you get on the ramp. You'll need them in the same position as you would for a regular kick turn.

As you approach the ramp, be sure to lean back so you stay on your board. Just as you come to a stop on the ramp, twist your shoulders and lift your front truck to initiate the kick turn. Be aware that you'll now go from leaning back to leaning forward. Timing this right is really important: do it too early and you'll continue to move up the ramp, making it difficult to complete the turn; do it too late and you'll have already started to come down the ramp backwards.

Once you can do this while approaching
the ramp at an angle, you'll want to try
heading straight onto the ramp. The key to
this is making the most of your upper body
to make sure you turn the full 180 degrees.
You can even rotate your shoulders a little
bit in the opposite direction before you
spin to get enough momentum to rotate
all the way round. If you want a challenge,
then try a frontside kick turn; it's harder to
rotate fully and stay balanced, but start by
approaching at an angle and work your
way up to the full 180 kick turn.

Throwing
DOWN

If you need a bit more speed than pushing alone provides then learning how to throw down can come in very handy. Whether you've got a small run up for a stair set, need to go a bit faster down a ramp, or just want to set off with a little extra flair, throwing down will be your go-to. This skill involves picking up speed by running with your board in your hand, then chucking it on the ground and jumping on it.

To begin with you need your board in the correct hand: left hand if you're regular, right hand if you're goofy. How many strides you decide to take will depend on how fast you want to go, but I'd suggest a short, light jog to start off with.

Grab the board with your thumb on the grip and your four fingers on the underside of your nose, holding your board slightly in front of you

Once you've hit your desired pace you need to release the board. You need to do this in a way that lets the board land flat on the ground, so move your hand forward a little as you're letting go. You also need to time the release so you can immediately put your front foot on the board, making sure that you let go on a stride where your back foot is ahead of you.

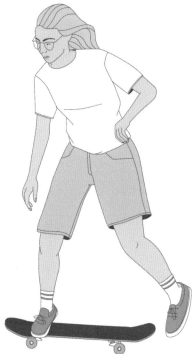

Keep your eyes on the board as you release it and try to place your front foot on the bolts before getting your back foot on. Jumping onto the board is the hardest part, so you may want to begin by throwing your board down and letting it roll along the ground a short distance before jumping on. You can work your way up to jumping straight on.

TRICKS

All you need to do is go on Instagram or YouTube and there are tons of clips of people doing the most insane tricks. This can either provide the perfect motivation to jump on your board and try something new, or make you feel like you'll never be as good as you want to be. Either way, it's important to know that for every trick you see someone land there are hundreds of failed attempts, plenty of slams and a load of simpler tricks that were learned to get to that point.

The only way to get anywhere near the ability of the best skaters is by starting with the basics, practising until you have perfected them, then moving on to something more difficult. All you need is your skateboard, some flat ground and determination. Once you're comfortable standing on your board, pushing and turning, it's time to learn some tricks so you can take your skating to the next level.

To begin with, give the tricks a go standing still, then try them while moving: if you keep at it, you'll get them eventually. Don't worry if you can only land a trick sloppily at first; it's generally accepted that if your feet don't touch the ground and you roll away then it counts. But just so you know, a clean landing is regarded as one where you land with your feet on the bolts. As you gain confidence and want to start doing some of these tricks down a flight of stairs or big drops, remember that landing on your bolts reduces the chance that you'll snap your deck. There's nothing worse than having to walk home holding a broken board. So, without further ado, let's start filling your bag of tricks!

Here are some tricks to get you started. There's a selection of flat-ground, rail/ledge and transition tricks, so there's plenty for you to practise.

HIPPY JUMP **68**

BODY VARIAL **72**

MANUAL **76**

PANCAKE FLIP **80**

OLLIE **84**

BACKSIDE POP SHOVE-IT **88**

FRONTSIDE POP SHOVE-IT **92**

FRONTSIDE 180 **96**

BACKSIDE 180 **100**

KICKFLIP **104**

HEELFLIP **108**

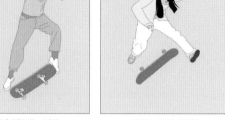

VARIAL KICKFLIP **112**

BACKSIDE BOARDSLIDE **116**

FRONTSIDE 50-50 **120**

ROCK TO FAKIE **124**

ROCK 'N' ROLL **130**

AXLE STALL **134**

FOOT POSITIONING

Make sure your feet are over the bolts. This ensures the board won't flick up as you jump.

Hippy JUMP

The idea of this trick is to jump off your skateboard into the air while your board continues to roll along the ground, then land back on your board. Some may argue that to do a real hippy jump you should jump over an obstacle while your skateboard passes underneath it, but I'd recommend practising without and gaining some confidence before giving that a go.

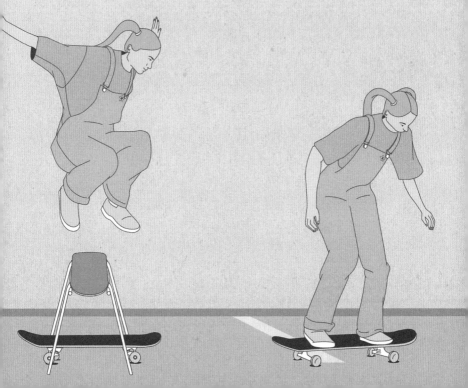

Hippy
JUMP

1. Act just like you would if you were to jump off the ground: bend your knees and get your arms in position. If you want to hippy jump over an obstacle, make sure you jump directly up and not forward, as this will cause your board to shoot backwards.

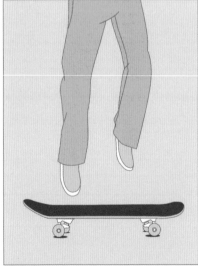

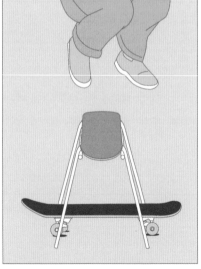

2. Extend your legs and jump off your toes so you can get as much height as possible. Lift your arms up to get yourself that little bit higher.

3. This part is crucial if you intend to go over an obstacle. Lift your knees up to your chest to get your feet as high as possible.

REMEMBER

Practise jumping over something that will move out of the way if you catch your feet on it. You could balance some pieces of wood on each other or get your mates to hold a piece of string.

When hippy jumping over something, the faster you go, the easier it will be. If you're going slowly, you'll need to be in the air for more time to clear the obstacle; if you go fast then you just need to jump high enough and you'll be sure to clear it.

4. Look back down at your board and aim to get your feet back onto your bolts. As you land, bend your knees to take some of the impact and ensure you can maintain your balance.

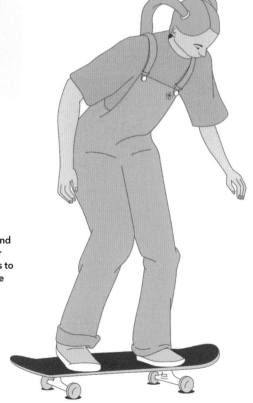

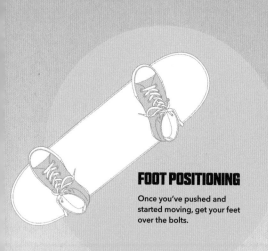

FOOT POSITIONING

Once you've pushed and started moving, get your feet over the bolts.

Body
VARIAL

This takes the hippy jump to the next level. Just like the previous trick, you have to jump off the board as it rolls along the ground, but with the addition of a 180-degree spin in the air. This can come in pretty useful – if you go up a ramp and come back down fakie, then you can do a quick body varial to make sure you're facing in the right direction again. Once you're feeling confident enough, you can try doing it over something or while on a ramp.

Body
VARIAL

REMEMBER

You can build up to the full 180 rotation by jumping halfway and putting your feet on the ground, either side of your board, before jumping back on.

Make sure you rotate frontside so you can still see where you're going when you rotate; a backside hippy jump might be a bit more difficult.

The hardest part about this trick is landing back on your board. Try starting with your shoulders as rotated as possible before you jump, so all you need to worry about is landing.

1. When you are moving, bend your knees so you're all set to jump in the air. Even at this point, your shoulders should begin to rotate.

2. As you jump, your shoulders should already have rotated about 90 degrees so you're facing forwards. The earlier you twist your shoulders, the easier it is to get all the way round.

3. When you reach peak height your legs should have twisted enough to meet your shoulders. From here on, your whole body is going to spin together.

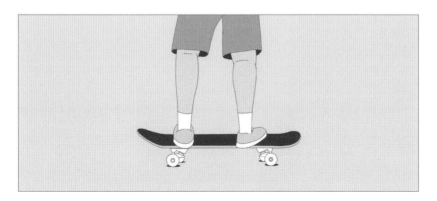

4. When you start to fall back down you should be looking at your board so you can aim your feet at the bolts. Try to land with both feet on the board at the same time and be sure to bend your knees, as this will aid your balance.

FOOT POSITIONING

Place your back foot on the tail with the ball of your foot in the middle of the board and your front foot on the bolts.

MANUAL

A manual is when you balance on the back two wheels of your skateboard. You can start by trying this trick while standing still and holding on to something, or even try doing it on grass or carpet first for a soft landing. Although it may appear to be a simple trick, holding it over long distances is most certainly not easy. Some of the best skaters will even do tricks into and out of manuals, but this takes years of practise. Once you're comfortable doing normal manuals, you can move into the nollie position and try a nose manual, or maybe attempt it in switch.

MANUAL

1. If you move your front foot closer to the tail it will be easier to lift up the front truck but harder to balance; you have to find perfect placement for yourself. If you're small it will be harder to lift the front truck, so changing your foot position will make things a little easier.

REMEMBER

Speed will make it easier to keep your balance and allow you to get further in a shorter amount of time.

Hold your arms up in the arm and use them to help you balance, like a tightrope walker.

When practising you can use cracks in the pavement or marks on the ground to see how far you can manual; set a personal record to try and beat, or maybe have a little competition with your mates.

2. Once your feet are in position, put some weight on your back foot and raise your front foot by bending your leg, similar to standing on one leg. Keep your body over the board - if you lean too far backwards you will fall back. Your centre of gravity should be over the back truck. To hold the manual you will have to keep adjusting how much you lean back and forth while trying to keep your centre of gravity over the back truck.

3. To stop manualling, take your weight off your back foot and lower your front foot to return the front wheels to the ground - although most of the time you'll reach a point where you can't hold the manual any longer and your front truck will drop to the ground. Remember that if your tail touches the ground while you're doing a manual then most consider the trick not to count.

FOOT POSITIONING

Get into position with your feet on the ground and the skateboard placed griptape down on top of your feet with your toes near the bolts. The board shouldn't cover the whole of your feet, just the toes.

Pancake FLIP

Flip tricks that are done while standing on your skateboard are hard to learn so the pancake flip is a great place to start. This is done by standing on the ground and resting the board on your feet, so it can't be done while moving. In this example the board only flips halfway, but if you're feeling confident you can try it with the board starting on its wheels and flip it all the way round.

Pancake
FLIP

1. Make sure you're in an open space as you might fall backwards when you're giving this a go and you don't want to bang your head on a wall. Get your feet into position. Bend your knees and jump slightly forward so that your toes hook the edge of the skateboard, flipping it over onto its wheels.

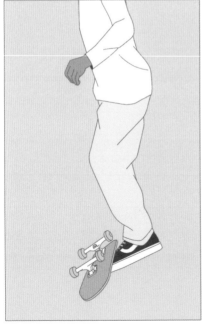

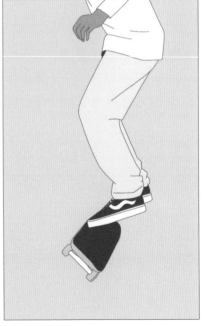

REMEMBER

To build your confidence you may want to begin by doing the flip with just one foot, making sure you can flip the board and get one foot on it before attempting to jump and land with both feet.

If you want to make things a bit harder, you can start with the wheels on the ground and try to flip the board the whole way round before landing on it.

2. While you're in the air, look for the bolts of the board and aim to get your feet onto them. It may take a few tries to get the board to flip just the right amount to land on it while it's flat. Remember that you and the board will land further forward than your starting position.

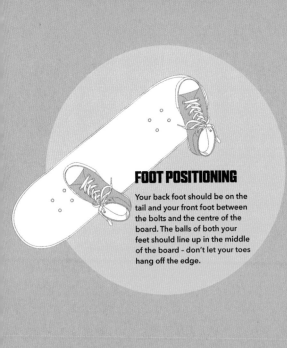

FOOT POSITIONING

Your back foot should be on the tail and your front foot between the bolts and the centre of the board. The balls of both your feet should line up in the middle of the board – don't let your toes hang off the edge.

OLLIE

This is a really important one as it is the basis for almost all flip tricks and grinds. As with everything you do on a skateboard, it takes a lot of practice to get right. It's a combination of a few movements, so if you're finding it difficult to do, practise the different stages one by one; if you're not getting one bit right then the rest will be tough. It's best to try each stage on the spot before attempting it while moving.

OLLIE

REMEMBER

Keep your body straight or the board will turn and it will be more difficult to land.

Don't lean back over the tail, and keep your body over the board. If you keep launching the board forward when you slide your foot up, then this will probably be the reason.

1. Ollies work by hitting the tail of the board off the ground: this is called popping the board. To do this you need to bend your knees and jump off your back foot, like you're hopping. Make sure you jump off

the ball of your foot: to see why that's necessary, try jumping off the ground with your feet flat - you won't get very high. Don't let your foot and the tail hit the ground together or the board won't pop.

2. Once you're able to pop the board off the ground you can start thinking about your other foot. You'll notice in the first stage that the board pops up at an angle. Now you need to use your front foot to straighten out the board. When the board has popped and is in the air, slide your front foot from the centre towards the nose. Run your foot along the middle of the board, not towards the edges or the board will spin.

3. Now that the board is flat in the air, you need to prepare to land. Keep your body directly over the board, and straighten your feet so they're flat on the top of the deck and wide apart.

4. As you land you may need to bend your knees a little to take the impact and help you keep your balance.

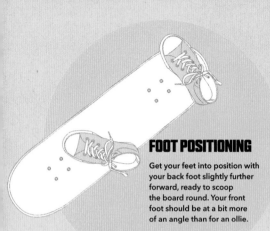

FOOT POSITIONING

Get your feet into position with your back foot slightly further forward, ready to scoop the board round. Your front foot should be at a bit more of an angle than for an ollie.

Backside Pop
SHOVE-IT
(SHUVIT)

Shove-its, both backside and frontside, are done by jumping and rotating the board 180 degrees. The crucial part for this trick is the scooping motion of the back foot. At first you might find it difficult to get the board to fully spin round, but that's okay – the hardest part is committing to landing on the board, so if you can pluck up the courage to jump and try to get both feet back on the board then you're on the right path.

Backside Pop
SHOVE-IT
(SHUVIT)

REMEMBER

To begin with, it may be easier to rotate the board so it lands a little further forward than you. This involves popping the board a little less and jumping slightly forward so that you land on the board.

Practise this trick on grass or carpet to gain some confidence before taking it onto hard ground.

Although the main action is with your back foot, you can use your front foot to guide the rotation of the board.

1. Before attempting the full trick it's important that you get the scooping motion down. This involves popping the board while dragging the tail behind you, allowing the board to come off the ground and creating the motion necessary to rotate the board. Practise this with your front foot on the ground and your back foot on the tail, making sure you get your back foot onto the board once it's fully rotated. Just like in an ollie, you need to do this with the ball of your foot, but your foot should be a little further forward. If you can master this motion then you're ready to get both feet on the board.

2. Now you've worked out what to do with your back foot, it's time to get your front foot on the board. Position it near the centre of the deck and put your back foot in the same position as before. Bend your knees, lift up your front foot and jump off your back foot while doing the scooping motion you've just practised. Don't lean back when doing this or the board will move away from you.

3. Once you've jumped and scooped you need to get your back foot back in position. Bring your front foot back up and in line with your back foot, ready to catch the board as it pops up. Make sure your feet are flat, so the board stays in position.

4. Once you've caught the board with your feet and you start to descend, bend your knees and brace for impact. At first you might not actually catch the board, so you need to think about where the board is going to land and aim for the bolts.

FOOT POSITIONING

Similar to a backside shove-it, except front foot should be slightly further forward and back foot slightly further back. The heel of your back foot should be hanging off the edge of the board.

Frontside Pop
SHOVE-IT

This is the same as a backside shove-it (see p88), but the board spins the opposite way round. Generally people learn this after they've learned the backside version, but some people find the frontside easier. Give it a go and see what you think.

Frontside Pop
SHOVE-IT

REMEMBER

When learning frontside shove-its it's essential that you start out by anticipating the board going a little behind you and jumping backwards onto it. It will be quite tough at first to pop the board directly up into your feet.

If you have an old deck without trucks or wheels, take it onto some carpet and practise this trick. This can really help you perfect the scoop motion and let you work out where the board will go when you pop it.

1. The heel of your back foot should be hanging off the edge of the board, as the popping action will be done with the ball of your foot. Start by putting your front foot on the ground and practising the popping motion. Slam your back foot down and away from you, causing the board to pop up and rotate 180 degrees. Make sure you don't clip your shins with your board and try to get your back foot back on the tail.

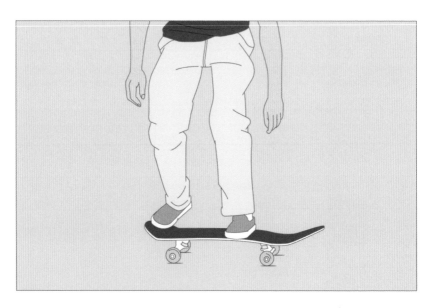

2. Let's put what you've learned into action. For this step, get your front foot into position on the board, bend your knees, and get ready on the balls of your feet. Lift your front foot while jumping off your back foot, and pop the tail down and away from you to get the board off the ground and rotating.

3. As the board spins round and pops up, you'll need to catch it with your front foot. You also need to get your back foot back in position on the board. If you can get it back in time, you can catch the board with both feet at the same time.

4. Once you've got the board under your feet, brace for impact. As the wheels hit the ground, bend your knees to maintain balance and roll away.

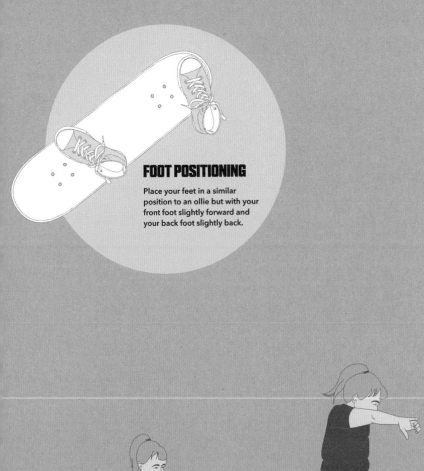

FOOT POSITIONING

Place your feet in a similar position to an ollie but with your front foot slightly forward and your back foot slightly back.

Frontside
180

180s are when your body and your board spins half a rotation. Just like a kick turn, or any trick that involves a body rotation, this trick is led by your shoulders. 180s are the foundation for a whole bunch of other tricks and always look good in a line so it's a great one to suss out. Frontside 180s are considered to be slightly easier, as you can keep an eye on where you're going as you do it.

Frontside
180

REMEMBER

See if you can do this off a small drop like a curb. Move alongside the edge and the drop will give you a bit of extra time to get the rotation in before you hit the ground.

You can learn to 180 in the same way you can learn to pop shove-it. Practise the motion by starting with your front foot on the ground and just working on your back foot and shoulder motion.

1. You need as much momentum as possible for this trick, so rotate your shoulders a little in the opposite direction to the way you're about to spin. Then, when you're ready, quickly spin your shoulders round.

2. Once the top half of your body has gone halfway round (facing in the direction that you're moving), your legs need to come into action. The motion is similar to that of a frontside pop shove-it. When you lift up your front foot, your backfoot needs to pop the tail against the ground, as you jump off your back leg and scoop the board round 180 degrees.

3. Your legs now need to spin round to catch up with the top half of your body. As your back foot sweeps the board round, your front foot can guide the movement of the other end of the deck. As you come to land your body should be aligned, or your top half may even have rotated more than your legs.

4. Once you and your board have done a full rotation you'll be coming back towards the ground. It's common for the board to land a little further back from where you started, but this is fine; as long as you end up standing on the board, you've got it!

FOOT POSITIONING

Begin with your feet in a
similar position to an ollie:
front foot between the centre
of the board and the bolts
and back foot on the tail, but
with your front foot slightly
back and your back foot
slightly forward.

Backside 180

The backside 180 is the same as the frontside one, but you'll rotate in the opposite direction, so that your back will face the direction of movement as you spin round. This may be a little more difficult, but remember that when you're moving you don't need to be exact, and even if you don't spin the full 180 degrees you can still roll away.

Backside
180

REMEMBER

If your foot keeps slipping off the board as you do the 180 then this could be down to your starting foot position. As you spin round your foot will slide across the board a little, so make sure you adjust your starting position accordingly.

If you can find a really smooth surface like wood or polished concrete, you may find it useful to practise this spinning motion without popping. See if you can get your legs and board 180 degrees round just by using your arms and shoulders while lifting up your front foot, then you just need to introduce the pop. The motion is similar to that of a powerslide (see p44).

1. Just like when doing a frontside 180, you will need as much momentum in the spin as possible. Do this by starting with your shoulders twisted slightly forward, in the opposite direction to the way they're about to spin.

2. Use your arms and shoulders to begin the rotation of the top half of your body. As you're about halfway round, with your body facing in the opposite direction to your movement, the bottom half of your body needs to do some work. While your body is rotating, begin the motion of an ollie with your legs. Raise your front leg while popping and jumping with your back leg. Unlike in an ollie, your back foot needs to go down and behind you, similar to a backside pop shove-it – this will cause the board to rotate.

3. The moment you've popped, your feet need to move the board round so it continues to rotate with the rest of your body. Your back foot will continue to move around while your front will guide the other end. Try to keep the board underneath you; if you lean too far either way, it will get away from you. As you reach maximum height your shoulders and legs should be aligned, or your legs may even have rotated further than your top half.

4. When learning this trick you may find it easier to aim to land a little further forward than where you take off. As you land make sure you bend your knees to aid your balance. You may also need to reshuffle your feet and readjust your shoulders in order to stay on the board.

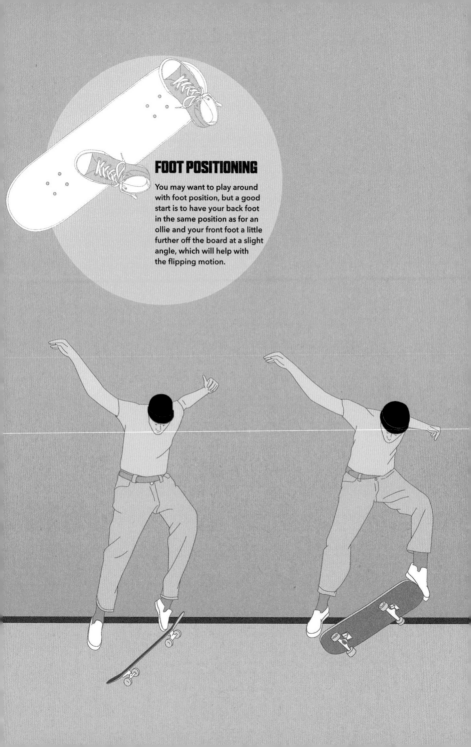

FOOT POSITIONING

You may want to play around with foot position, but a good start is to have your back foot in the same position as for an ollie and your front foot a little further off the board at a slight angle, which will help with the flipping motion.

KICKFLIP

There are two widely known things about skateboarding, even for people with no real interest in it: firstly, that Tony Hawks is a skateboarder, and secondly, that a kickflip is a trick. If you walk around with a skateboard under your arm for long enough, it's almost guaranteed that someone will shout 'DO A KICKFLIP'. Learning a kickflip is no easy feat and it's perfectly normal for it to take months or even years to land. This trick involves doing an ollie, but using the toes of your front foot to flip the board round before landing back on it. It may take time to get, but the feeling of landing your first ever one is unrivalled.

KICKFLIP

REMEMBER

If your board seems to go too far away from you to be able to land on then you may be leaning too far backwards. Try to keep your shoulders centred over the board to avoid this happening. Similarly, don't lean too far forward or it will make it much more difficult to get your front foot on the board.

The kicking motion is just as much about being able to flick your foot as it is about kicking your leg. The further you kick your leg out, the further you have to get it back again, so make the most of the power you can get from flicking your foot.

1. This trick begins the same as an ollie, by bending your knees, lifting your front foot, popping the board and jumping off your back foot. Practise the jump/kick motion and try to land with only your front foot on the board. You may find that your front foot is the hardest one to get on your board, and this may be because you're kicking your foot downwards; try to kick it directly forwards instead. Once you can get your front foot on the board, try getting both feet on at the same time. You might need to jump a little higher and lift your back leg up.

2. As you jump up, you need to flip the board. When you ollie, you slide your front foot straight up the board, but when you kickflip you need to slide your foot off the edge of the board. Using the part of your shoe near your middle toe, you need to flick the nose of the board between the tip of the nose and the edge of the board.

3. At this point you need to get both feet in position to land on the board. Lift your back foot up by bending your back knee so it's over the board. Also retrieve your front foot from where you've kicked it and place it back over the board, so it's in position over the front bolts.

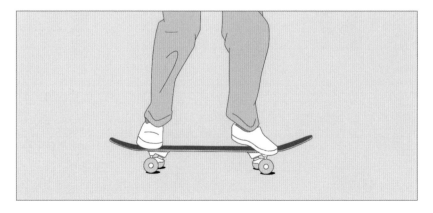

4. Once you've got both of your feet back over the bolts the hard part is done, and you can land back on the ground on top of your board. Bend your knees to take the impact and raise your clenched fists into the air triumphantly.

FOOT POSITIONING

Place your front foot between the bolts and the centre of the board with your toes hanging a little over the far edge of the board. Your back foot should be in the ollie position or a little further back.

HEELFLIP

This is the slightly less coveted sister of the kickflip, and whether or not it's easier or more difficult is down to personal experience. It's done by flipping the board the other way to a kickflip. Instead of sliding your foot off the side nearest to your body, you make the board flip by sliding it off the side that's furthest away. Although it's called a heelflip, the flipping action is actually done with the side of the foot, around the area of your little toe.

HEELFLIP

1. Just like in an ollie, raise your front foot, pop and jump off your back leg. Be sure that as you pop and jump you're already starting to slide your foot off the board. It's all one smooth movement. Working out the timing for each part takes some practice.

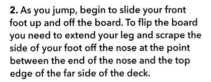

2. As you jump, begin to slide your front foot up and off the board. To flip the board you need to extend your leg and scrape the side of your foot off the nose at the point between the end of the nose and the top edge of the far side of the deck.

3. Once the board begins to spin, you need to get your feet in a position to catch the board. Lift your back foot up and bring it over the back of the board, over the back truck. Your front foot will be further away, so getting it back over the front bolts will be more of a challenge. You might have to lift your knees up quite a lot to get both feet on the board if it pops up high.

4. Once you've got both feet over the bolts you can catch the board and come back down to the ground. As you land, bend your knees to take the impact and help with your balance. Sometimes you'll find that your feet aren't quite in the perfect position, so you may have to adjust your body position to stay on the board and give you time to readjust your feet.

REMEMBER

Just as with kickflips, the main challenge of a heelflip can be getting your front foot back on the board. To work on this you can practise the pop, jump and flip while trying to get your front foot on the board; let your back foot land on the ground. Once you can consistently get your front foot on, try getting both feet on again.

FOOT POSITIONING

Place your back foot in the same position as for a backside pop shove-it: on the tail, but further forward, ready to scoop back. Front foot should be in a position similar to that for a kickflip, angled but a bit further onto the board.

Varial KICKFLIP

This is your first introduction to a trick that combines flipping the board and rotating it. Put simply, this trick is a backside pop shove-it and a kickflip done simultaneously, so it will help a lot if you can do these tricks, although people have been known to get varials before learning to kickflip. Along with pushing mongo, this trick is also subject to some skateboarding snobbery. Some people think it's not a particularly good-looking trick, but others say if popped and caught well, it deserves their respect. Either way, this is a great one to learn as it opens the door to other tricks.

Varial KICKFLIP

REMEMBER

Although this is a kickflip and pop shove-it combined, your front foot will actually go straight forward as when doing an ollie. This is because the board will have already rotated a little by the time you fling your front foot forward to spin the board. If you're struggling to get the board to spin, start with your foot a little lower down the board.

1. As with other tricks that require the board to rotate, you may find you need to adjust where you jump to account for the movement of the board. When doing varial flips your board might move a little forward, so to land on the bolts, you'll have to move forward too. Now bend your knees, raise your front foot, pop and scoop your back foot behind you.

2. As you scoop the board around with your back foot, you should begin to slide your front foot forward. Your front leg should move directly away from your back leg so that as the board rotates your foot flicks the edge of the board around the area of your front bolts. If done right, the board should fully spin by the time it has done its 180-degree rotation.

3. At this point both of your feet have moved in different directions away from the board, so you need to pull them back in and lift your knees up to get your feet over the board. Keep your eyes down on the board so you know where to aim and place your feet over the bolts.

4. Once you've got your feet over the bolts, catch the board as you start to come back towards the ground. Remember, you might need to jump a little forward to land back on the board. As you get more comfortable, you can try and pop them directly up.

FOOT POSITIONING

Start out in the same foot position as the ollie.

Backside BOARDSLIDE

This is your first introduction to the world of slides. These tricks involve getting onto an obstacle, like a ledge or a rail, and sliding along it on your deck. The tricks vary depending on whether it's your nose, tail or the centre of the board that you balance on, and how you approach the obstacle. For a backside grind/slide you have to approach an obstacle so that it's alongside your back. For a boardslide you need to raise your front truck up and over the obstacle. For both it's important that you can ollie high enough to get onto whatever it is you want to slide along.

Backside BOARDSLIDE

REMEMBER

To begin with, try to do a very short boardslide by mounting the obstacle right at the end so you only slide about a foot before you come to the end of it. You may not be able to rotate fully back to your starting position when you land but, even if you only twist halfway back round, you should be able to roll away, just a bit slower than preferable.

Getting onto an obstacle, especially a rail, can be quite daunting. The hardest part is committing. One thing that does help, but you might not want to hear, is going faster. Speed helps you slide cleanly, and makes it easier to balance while improving your chances of rolling away.

1. The first thing to consider is how you approach the obstacle, and this will differ depending on whether it's a rail or a ledge. For a ledge, an angled approach works well as it helps you lock onto it, whereas for a rail a more parallel approach may be better as rails give less resistance and you don't want to slide right over it. You also need to consider speed: if you're not going fast enough then you won't slide, let alone make it off the end. As you come closer to your target, prepare to do a 90-degree ollie, bend your knees and prepare to twist your shoulders.

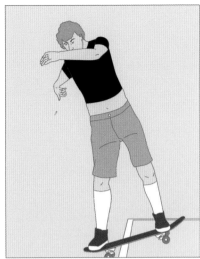

2. Once you're close enough to get onto the obstacle, perhaps about a foot away, begin to ollie. Raise your front foot, pop and jump - but most importantly, open up your body, rotating your shoulders so that your legs and board will rotate 90 degrees.

3. As you land on the obstacle it's important to lean back slightly. How much you have to lean back depends on the surface of the obstacle; rough materials like concrete will provide more resistance, so you'll need to lean back more to push the board through the slide. Round rails, marble ledges or anything with lots of wax will be buttery and provide far less resistance, so you won't need to lean back much at all. Once you're sliding, your next challenge is getting off, so start to rotate your arms and shoulders back towards your starting position.

4. When you reach the end of the obstacle you'll naturally drop off it, but you need to make sure you'll roll away. With your shoulders already rotated, you should get the momentum you need to twist your legs so the board comes off the obstacle and returns to a position necessary to land. You also need to lean a little more forward, especially if you've been leaning quite far back, so when you land on the flat you don't slip back. Once you're off, get ready to bend your knees and take the impact.

FOOT POSITIONING

Start out in the same foot position as the ollie.

Frontside 50-50

It's time for your first grind. Grinds are done by moving along an obstacle with your trucks in contact with it. Just like slides, tricks differ depending on the position of the trucks on the ledge, rail or coping, and how you approach it. A 50-50 is when you move along an obstacle with both of your trucks on it. This is a frontside 50-50, so you'll approach the obstacle so that it's alongside your front. This may be a little more difficult than a backside boardslide as you need to ollie high enough to get right on top of the obstacle with both your front and back trucks.

Frontside
50-50

REMEMBER

Trucks don't move as easily across rough surfaces as boards do, so if you're planning to do this on something concrete, make sure you lather it with wax or you won't get very far.

Note that it's much more difficult to balance when doing a 50-50 on a round rail. Start out on a ledge or square rail, which are much easier to lock on to.

The faster you're going, the easier it is to get out of the grind because you need to hold the front truck up for less time in order to drop off the end and land on the ground with both trucks hitting the ground at the same time.

1. Approach the obstacle at a slight angle. You need to make sure that your momentum will take you onto it once you've ollied. If you're skating parallel to the obstacle it will be quite tricky to get your board and weight over it. Ensure you have enough speed for the distance you want to grind, taking into account how easily you'll grind across the surface. Make sure you keep the top half of your body side-on to the rail or ledge. Get your feet in position to ollie and bend your knees, ready to pop.

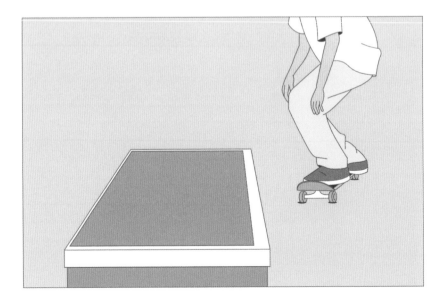

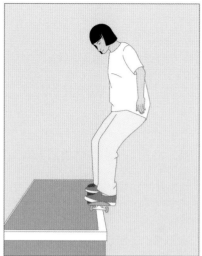

2. Timing your ollie is important: too early and you won't make it onto the obstacle, too late and you'll overshoot it. The same goes for the height of your ollie so it may take quite a few attempts just to get the timing and height right. When you're about a foot or so away from the obstacle pop your ollie.

3. As you're in the air you need to readjust slightly – you're currently at an angle, so you need to straighten out. Move your back foot slightly towards the obstacle and your front foot slightly back. You want both your trucks to land at about the same time. As you land, lean slightly back so that your wheels rest right against the edge of the obstacle; this helps you lock into the grind and makes it much easier to balance.

4. As you near the end of your obstacle you need to make sure you lift the front truck before it drops off the end. Put some pressure on the tail and lift up your front foot, similar to a manual (or in this case a 5-0 grind). Once your back truck drops off the end of the obstacle, lower your front foot so the board is flat and you can land on both trucks at the same time. Bend your knees to absorb the shock, and roll away.

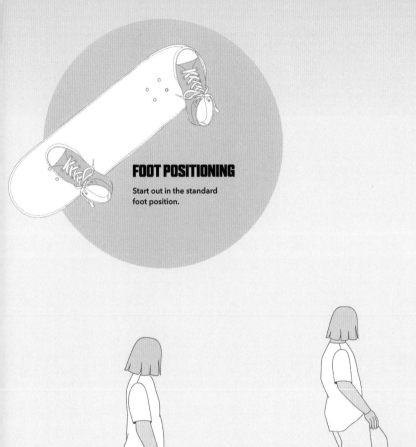

FOOT POSITIONING

Start out in the standard foot position.

Rock to FAKIE

If you prefer the idea of skating bowls more than stairs and rails then it's essential you learn some transition tricks. This one provides the perfect initiation into skating quarter pipes and will be your first trick on the coping. This is a type of stall, a trick that involves resting briefly on the coping of the ramp before going back down. As with most tricks, there are slight variations in the way you can do this, and as you progress you'll want to develop your own style, but this is a good way to start.

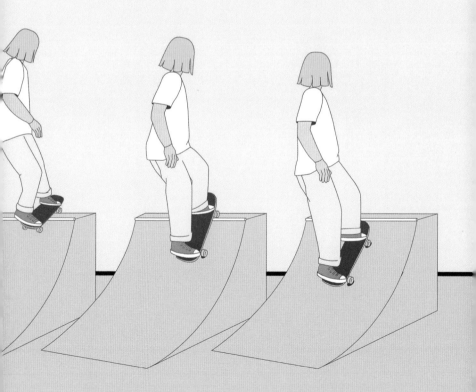

Rock to
FAKIE

1. Make sure you approach the ramp with enough distance to gauge how much speed you need and to get your feet in position. You'll need your back foot on the tail and your front foot over the bolts. The further back your back foot is, the more control you'll have over lifting up the front of the deck. The further forward your front foot is, the easier it will be to balance as you go up and down the ramp.

REMEMBER

Getting the right amount of speed is crucial to this trick. If you go really fast, your front truck might continue quite far past the coping; this is fine, but you'll have more of a challenge getting back down as you'll have to hold your front truck up for longer. You may get so much speed that your back truck goes over the coping, and you'll have to start over. If you don't get enough speed then your front truck won't reach the coping.

Keep your shoulders square over the board; there will be very little, if any, rotation of the shoulders during this trick. If you approach the ramp with your shoulders facing forward then you'll face difficulties when coming back down the ramp fakie.

2. As you go up the ramp, don't shift your weight forward as you would when you normally go up a ramp; make sure you lean back. The steeper the ramp, the more you will have to lean back. Even though your front truck will go over the coping, it's important you don't shift your weight forward. Keep your knees bent so you can balance more easily.

3. Raise your foot so the front truck can go over the coping. As your front truck approaches the coping, you need to lift your front foot up so that your front truck comes off the ramp and can go over the coping. Bend your front leg and straighten your back leg a little. The action is very similar to doing a manual.

Rock to
FAKIE

3. Once your front truck is over the coping, lower your front truck so it rests above the coping. Straighten your front leg and bend your back leg. Remember that this movement is all in the legs so don't shift your shoulders forward or it will be near impossible to stay on your board as you come back down.

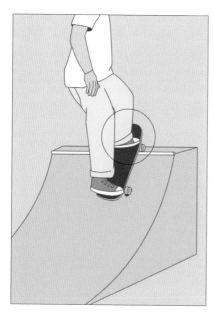

4. You're now going to go back down the ramp. Twist your head and look down the ramp so you can see where you're about to go. Bend your front leg and straighten your back leg, lifting up your front truck and releasing yourself off the coping and back down into the ramp. This is the toughest part as it takes a lot of courage to trust your ability to pull it off.

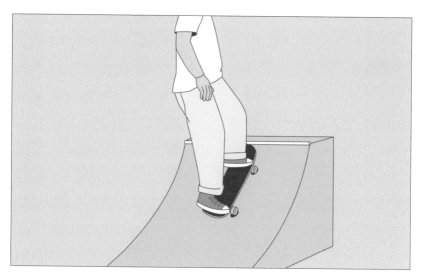

5. Make sure you keep that front truck up until you've cleared the coping. If your truck clips the coping, you'll hang up: your board will stop, and you'll keep going. Once it's past the coping, bring the front truck back down to the ramp and roll away.

FOOT POSITIONING

Start out in the standard foot position.

Rock 'n' ROLL

This trick is the next step on from a rock to fakie and involves turning 180 degrees and coming back down the ramp in your normal stance, rather than going backwards. The first few steps are identical to a rock to fakie as you will do the same stall, but things differ from there. Some people find this one a little less scary as you'll end up facing the direction in which you're moving so hanging up and falling backwards isn't as much of a worry.

Rock 'n'
ROLL

REMEMBER

The part of this trick people have most difficulty with is the rotation. Be prepared to use your arms and shoulders to shift the top half of your body all the way round so you can get back down the ramp.

As with a rock to fakie, there are different ways to do this, and eventually you'll find your own favourite. When learning this I suggest getting enough speed so that your front truck goes just over the coping. Some people like to deck out this trick so you go so far over that your back truck reaches the coping, but that's much more difficult.

1. Push and get enough speed to get your front truck over the coping. Consider the shape/size of the ramp when working out how fast to go. Make sure you stop pushing at a sufficient distance to be able to get your feet into position. As you go up the ramp, lean back, away from the ramp. Keep your knees bent and be ready to lean further back on steeper ramps.

2. Now that your front truck has gone over the coping, lower your front foot. If you got the right amount of speed, this should happen as you naturally come to a stop. As soon as you place your front truck over the coping you should already be rotating your shoulders to come down the ramp. With your front foot planted securely you should be able to get your shoulders right round.

3. As you lift your front foot up, the momentum of the top half of your body should help you spin your board round. This part is very similar to a kick turn, pivoting on the wheels of your back truck. You can get extra momentum by pushing off your front leg as you begin the turn.

4. Once you've rotated 180 degrees, the wheels of your front truck should come into contact with the ramp. Be prepared to bend your knees to take a little impact and make sure you lean forward into the ramp.

FOOT POSITIONING

Start out in the standard
foot position.

Axle
STALL

This is another great transition trick and involves stalling on the coping on both trucks. Speed, timing, and weight distribution are all key to getting this one right. Just like other transition tricks, it's best to start out on a smaller quarter pipe, so you can finesse the technique before taking it onto something bigger. There are lots of little variations to the way you can do an axle stall, but this is a good place to start. For proper technique it's important to get right on top of the ramp before coming back in.

Axle
STALL

REMEMBER

1. Push so you get enough speed to get your back truck up to the coping. This means you'll need to go a bit quicker than you do for a rock to fakie or rock 'n' roll. Some people prefer to approach the ramp at a slight angle so they don't need to turn as much, but your momentum can carry off the coping. It might be easier to approach it straight on.

When people first attempt this trick they often find themselves landing in a feeble stall, which is when the front truck lands top of the ramp rather than on the coping. This could happen for a number of reasons: you could be shifting your weight forward too soon, you might not be holding the front truck up for long enough, or perhaps you're not getting your shoulders round quick enough.

Dropping back in from an axle stall can be scary but, just like when dropping in, it's really important to make sure you lean forward enough and get your body down the ramp so that you can roll away properly. If you like, you can place your board on the coping and practise going back in before trying the whole trick together.

2. As you get onto the ramp, lean back and keep your legs bent to maintain balance. Lift your front foot up as your front truck approaches the coping and continue to move up the ramp. You need to maintain your body position for the time being, leaning back.

3. Timing here is critical. As your back truck is just about to hit the coping, swiftly twist your shoulders 90 degrees and shift your body weight onto the ramp so you end up standing upright on your skateboard at the top of the ramp with both trucks resting on the coping.

Axle
STALL

4. Depending on how you've landed on the coping, you may want to readjust your trucks at this point. Some find it easier to come back into the ramp when their back truck is pushed forward so that the wheel on the top of the ramp is pushed up against the coping. You may be able to get straight into this position or you may prefer to keep the truck fully on the ramp

5. To go back into the ramp you need to pivot on your back foot. Twist your shoulders first then lift up your front foot, bringing your front truck off the coping and back into the ramp. You now need to transfer your weight back into the ramp, and lower your front shoulder so your body moves back down the ramp.

6. As you land you want to make sure you've rotated the full 90 degrees and that you are leaning far enough forward to balance on the ramp. As your front wheels hit the ramp your legs should be bent enough to take impact so you can roll away. As you move further down the ramp, readjust your weight to stay on your board as you come down the slope.

GLOSSARY

180 (one-eighty)
A trick that involves a half rotation of your body and your skateboard.

50-50
A grind in which both trucks are in contact with the obstacle.

Backside (obstacle)
Describes a trick that is done on an obstacle that is behind you as you approach it.

Backside (trick)
A trick that is done by rotating the body or the board, so that the back of your body faces the direction of movement (apart from when doing tricks fakie).

Bank
A large, flat, angled ramp, often with a platform at the top.

Boardslide
A trick done on an obstacle in which you move along the obstacle with the centre of the board in contact with it.

Bolts
The hardware used to attach your board to your trucks.

Bowl
A large cement structure, based on an empty swimming pool, normally sunken in the ground, which is used for skateboarding.

Complete
A skateboard sold with all the components necessary to use it.

Concave
The curve on the surface of a deck.

Coping
The concrete/metal part that runs along the top edge of a ramp, commonly found on bowls, quarter pipes and half pipes.

Cruiser
A skateboard primarily intended for transport. It may have large, soft wheels and a smaller shaped deck.

Deck
The long, flat, wooden part of a skateboard.

Double kick
A skateboard with both a long tail and nose, which can be used to perform tricks.

Dropping in
A manoeuvre in which you place the tail of your board at the top end of a ramp and the back truck over the edge in order to go down it. Usually done on a ramp with coping.

Fakie
When you ride your skateboard in your normal stance, but backwards with the tail of your board pointing in the direction of travel.

Flip trick
A manoeuvre that requires you to fully rotate the board, causing the grip tape to face down and then back up again. Examples include kickflips and heelflips.

Freestyle
A style of skateboarding in which you perform technical tricks on flat ground.

Frontside (obstacle)
A trick that is done on an obstacle that you face as you approach it.

Frontside (trick)
A trick that is done by rotating your body or board so that the back of your body faces the direction of movement (apart from when doing tricks fakie).

Goofy
One of two preferred stances. Goofy skaters prefer moving with their right foot at the front of the board and their left foot at the back. (See also Regular.)

Grind box
A relatively short obstacle with hard edges built for doing grinds on, typically wider than a ledge.

Grind
A manoeuvre that involves moving across an obstacle while one or both of the trucks is in contact with it.

Grip tape
The sandpaper-like material stuck to the top of a deck that makes it easier to keep your feet on the board.

Hanging up
The action of catching a truck on the coping of a ramp causing you to fall off your board.

Kick turn
Changing direction by lifting up your front truck and pivoting on the back truck.

Ledge
A narrow grind box, sometimes connected to the side of another ramp.

Line
Either a number of tricks done in quick succession, or a route one typically takes through a skatepark.

Longboard
A long skateboard, typically with large, soft wheels.

Manual
A trick done by balancing on the wheels of one truck.

Mongo
Pushing with your front foot rather than your back foot.

Nollie
A stance in which you place your front foot on the nose of your board and your back foot nearer the centre. Also, an ollie done with your feet in this position.

Nose
The top end of your skateboard.

Obstacle
A structure used for performing tricks when skateboarding.

Ollie
A trick that involves jumping and getting your skateboard in the air by slamming the tail against the ground.

Manual (Manny) pad
A relatively small, flat obstacle typically used for performing manuals on.

Pop
The act of slamming the tail or nose of your skateboard against the ground to get the whole board in the air.

Powerslide
A method of slowing down or stopping by rotating your board 90 degrees and sliding across the ground.

Quarter pipe
A curved ramp, typically with coping on the top edge.

Rail
A thin metal obstacle used for grinds and slides.

Regular
One of two preferred stances. Regular skaters prefer moving with their left foot at the front of the board and their right foot at the back. (See also Goofy.)

Rolling in
Entering a ramp by moving from the flat top directly onto the ramp

Shove-it (aka Shuvit)
A manoeuvre that requires you to rotate the board while keeping the grip tape facing up.

Slalom
A style of skateboarding that involves going down hills and weaving around cones.

Slide
A manoeuvre that involves moving across an obstacle while the nose, tail or centre of the board are in contact with it.

Stall
A trick that involves going up a ramp and holding a static position on the coping before coming back into the ramp.

Street skating
A style of skateboarding that involves skating obstacles such as stairs, rails and ledges. This can be done in a skatepark or in the urban environment.

Switch
Skating the opposite to your preferred stance: for example, goofy, if you prefer regular.

Tail
The bottom end of your skateboard.

Throwing down
Getting on your skateboard by running, releasing the board and jumping on it.

Transition
The style of skateboarding that involves skating obstacles such as quarter pipes, half pipes and bowls. Also, the part of a ramp that curves from horizontal to vertical.

Truck
The metal part of the skateboard that the wheels and deck are fixed to.

Vert skating
A style of skateboarding done on a large half pipe which is typically at least 3.4m (11ft) and vertical at the top of the ramp.

Acknowledgements

Thanks to everyone at Skittledog. Ewa Zak created these incredible illustrations and was so attentive to the minor details; without your pictures, the words would be nothing. Gaynor Sermon guided me through the writing of this book and explained every stage of the process to me - thanks for your support and patience. Thank you to Masumi Briozzo for making every page pop; to Angus Hyland for your creative genius and to Felicity Awdry for making it all happen. Your work didn't go unnoticed, and I really appreciate everything you put into this.

A huge thanks to Zara Larcombe for making this whole project possible, from a suggestion while clapping on the doorstep during lockdown to the publishing of an actual book - I still can't quite get my head around it. I can't thank you enough.